ALL FOR THE
LOVE
OF
HORSES

PATTI DAMMIER

All for the Love of Horses

iUniverse books may be ordered through booksellers or by contacting:

iUniverse
1663 Liberty Drive
Bloomington, IN 47403
www.iuniverse.com
844-349-9409

Because of the dynamic nature of the Internet, any web addresses or links contained in this book may have changed since publication and may no longer be valid. The views expressed in this work are solely those of the author and do not necessarily reflect the views of the publisher, and the publisher hereby disclaims any responsibility for them.

Library of Congress Control Number: 2022910897
ISBN: 978-1-6632-3943-3 (sc)
ISBN: 978-1-6632-3944-0 (e)

Print information available on the last page.

iUniverse rev. date: 07/19/2022

CONTENTS

Horses should be trained in such a way that they not only love their riders but look forward to the time they are with them.

Xenophon 400 B.C.

PREFACE

Our final home

History and life tend to repeat continually. Anyone who has lived an adult life for at least two decades will observe this fact. This story began in a small community on rural Long Island, continued to Europe, and returned to the United States to the place that was a dream wish. It was always a vision to be able to look out and see my beloved horses, and not have to worry about finding the next boarding stable, even though this was to take an enormous effort.

Our lives eventually become the product of our history and experiences with the sometimes-random possibilities of those we encounter who influence our ideas. I maintain that everything one needs to learn about groups may be learned at a riding club, or any club for that matter, and those members we gravitate toward, as part of our important decisions.

This is mostly a story about horses, but it is impossible to extricate all the other surroundings and happenings. Two of the horses that I own/owned came about because of difficult economic and political occurrences and not solely by my perseverance and timely decisions. Of course, these factors were important, but without the random possibilities they wouldn't have occurred. They came about more than twenty years apart, but both these horses had a wonderful life because of those economic happenings and the devoted horse lovers who intervened. The first horse that I was lucky to own because of these events was the Portuguese Lusitano stallion Xierxo, and the second was the Russian Orlov-Rostopchin stallion Firefox.

Horses until the close of the end of the Second World War had a rough time and if it weren't for humans who rescued these ancient breeds, the breeding lines would have been lost forever. I contend that horses in the last seventy years have had to be rescued for the less obvious outcomes of war but rather the recent economic influences that have also had an insidious effect on horses and their owners. These happenings weren't noticed or substantially reported because they didn't occur with large groups and with any significant reporting; they ended in the demise of many wonderful horses and their breeding lines, which were the results.

This story is about all the wonderful horses and the people who love them…their stories should be told to redeem what has been forgotten.

CHAPTER 1

War Dancer: The Beginning of the Story

Nanny, please don't eat Mommy's fruit trees!

Something kept calling me from my childhood; my love of animals and horses. There was no way of knowing what was ahead for me as I threw down that lifeless tennis racket for the last time. The only reason I played the uninspiring game was to be with friends.

We always had cats, dogs, and other animals that found their way to our home. The Easter visit to my aunt in the city yielded from a garbage can, six cute fluffy chicks. The cute chicks, however, grew up and turned into six loudly crowing roosters every morning. The property was large enough for many animals and a nice place had been built for the new adoptees but their new found voices carried a great distance. Needless to say our neighbors, who even though not near, were very unhappy, especially on holidays when they didn't have to get up. There were many farms in the area, and because of the loud crowing, the roosters had to be taken to the nearby chicken farm where they would have plenty of friends, so it was said.

Then there was Nanny, surely not an original name for a goat. We were taking care of Nanny, and soon found out why they didn't ask for Nanny back. She ate everything in sight. She had eaten the bark off all of my mother's carefully planted fruit trees and started on our log cabin playhouse. When Nanny started chewing on the walls of an addition my father was building on the back of our house, Nanny had worn out her visitor's welcome and was unceremoniously returned to her owners.

Along came the animal that changed my life. My father took this pet in trade for some work he did on a neighbor's car. My brother, while recuperating from an auto accident, had to stay on the ground and out of trees, off of bikes, and away from all the things a nine-year-old likes to do. He was supposed to be kept occupied with taking care of this yearling and staying out of mischief. As fate would have it, War Dancer became my responsibility and the beginning of a lifelong love for horses.

Throwing that tennis racket down gave me the clarity of mind that made me realize that after all these years of trying many different sports, I wanted to be with my first love…horses.

What better place than sunny Spain where horses abound? This was the start of an adventure that would take me over the main highways and back roads of Spain, Portugal, Germany, and England. We would escape from Spain with its terrible deathly horse sickness disease, which almost shut down the equestrian Olympic events, to the United States; then to Germany, and finally to return after over twenty-seven years to our own farm in the United States.

CHAPTER 2

Bobby-A and Horse Trading

Spanish spring Jerez Feria

When I was a youngster, riding along the powerline roads was fun. War Dancer merely consented to have me along as a passenger, and occasionally agreed to do as I wanted; more often he got his own way and would unceremoniously turn suddenly and off I slid. He would then stop and turn around and stare at me, as if to say, "You're not supposed to be there." I'd get back on and we'd gallop along nicely only to repeat the whole episode again. So that's how I learned to ride, bareback with my scarcely horse-sized pony.

After all these years I wondered if I would remember anything at all. The Rota Naval Station had several clubs and the stable club was located near where I worked teaching school. The navy base had a riding club, so that's when the sailors had enough of being rocked around on a ship they could come and rent a horse and get a little more of the same.

The horses were lined up in order of Western ridden horses and those ridden English style. I chose one of the only two English ridden mounts, Bobby-A since Western riding was clearly more popular among the sailors. These two horses didn't know how lucky they were. Also, when the ships came in, I always had a horse to rent. The other horses could only be taken out so many times to allow for a little rest and relaxation between the gallops in Marlborough country. The two English horses got plenty of rest and relaxation, because no one wanted to ride them because of the English saddles; no horn to hang on to. And it didn't look cool.

An American living in the area, called Chuck by the Americans and Carlos by the Spaniards, had a horse finder's fee. For ten bucks he would take you to all the local places that raised and sold horses. He was knowledgeable about the local area and knew the horse industry, including occasional stints with the Western movies being locally produced. The horse trade was a small group and Chuck knew all the maneuvering necessary.

I tracked him down and we were soon on our way to a local Spanish farm. Nothing would have prepared me for the places we would see and the way horses are kept and treated in Spain. Since that time, I saw beautiful places where horses are kept in large airy boxes and handled gently, but these places were few in the mostly farming area. One of the exceptional stables nearby in Jerez, is the stable of Alvaro Domecq. This was finally turned into the National Equestrian School of Jerez. In the near future I was able to study with the talented Portuguese dressage trainer who was the head trainer.

Most horses are kept tied in tiny, unclean stalls and never get to glimpse the light of day unless some buyer was coming to see them, or it was the time of the spring parades, called *Ferias*. This was my first lesson in Spanish horse trading, which seems to be an international sport. There was much to learn. I did understand and speak Spanish, but being a small foreigner is considered fair game. Whether you speak Spanish or not is irrelevant unless you're from that *Barrio* or local area. Carlos was one of them. Eventually I learned some tricks of my own. No matter how well you learn Spanish, you'll always be a foreigner someplace unless you stay right in your own little village. This is true of many places the world over.

Chuck decided I should get my feet wet, so I did the talking and a small, bedraggled animal was brought out. We were told this animal was no more than two years old and in excellent health. The price was twenty thousand pesetas, which was around two thousand dollars. He would have been lucky to get two hundred dollars at the local *Mercado*. Chuck, up to this point had, I think, purposely said nothing. He leaned over and opened the horse's mouth. The Spanish words flowed furiously and fast between Chuck and the local. The next thing I knew we were driving back down the nonexistent road we came in on. "Now," Chuck said, "we will have a chance of seeing something worthwhile and at reasonable prices." I asked him what he had said to the local. My parents had several acres with one small-sized horse and some pets that became a huge horse ranch in Texas where I grew up with horses and obviously could tell the difference between a two-year-old and a horse pushing twenty. It sounded so impressive in Spanish with all of the yelling and hand waving that it lost something in the translation. This lesson was learned well, and used especially effectively later, many times.

This was the beginning of the quest to seriously learn to ride. After asking around, one of my fellow teachers recommended an Englishman that taught history and equitation at a two-year college in Seville. We were to make many interesting friends, including many wonderful horses and people who spent much of their time caring for them.

CHAPTER 3

Mr. Jefferies

Several steeds shine in saddle show

Out of respect, our riding teacher during class was called Mr. Jefferies. He was a brilliant teacher; however, he repulsed most Spaniards because he suffered from Parkinson's disease. As far as their limited equestrian knowledge, anyone who shook like that couldn't possibly teach riding. Their image of a riding teacher was some young, dark-haired lad who looked like he just came out of the bullring.

Mr. Jefferies' approach came from a solid background riding and judging in England. He was excellent on the ground as he conveyed everything a rider needed to know with his wonderful British accent. Not only did the riders heed the master's voice, but the horses did as well. This was unfathomable for the young Spanish boys who were the grooms and already knew how to ride. They would joke and laugh behind his back. It was completely incomprehensible that riding was an art, and what they did with horses was merely shear brute force.

During my time in Spain, I was to fight these ideas first vocally, because I was outraged at the primitive techniques still being used, such as the *cerreta*, a curved piece of iron with small teeth that pressed around the nose. It wasn't uncommon to see beautiful horses in Andalusia with scarred noses. Thank heaven this technique has lost ground and at least the teeth are now wrapped to protect the nose. This tradition has been passed on by word of mouth since there wasn't information about other techniques, especially in small little villages where men prove themselves on horseback. This was to change as the written material of France, Austria, and Germany, with several hundred years of classical training, was translated. One of the first books that appeared in Spanish tack shops was from the head rider Podhajsky of the famous Austrian Spanish Riding School.

Obviously Jeff, as we now called him, didn't fit the image of a dominating male on horseback. It probably explains why so few Spanish women rode. Most of Jeff's students were foreigners, such as me and a few Spanish girls who were sent to learn English. This was changing and the Spanish riding school of Jerez had a talented female rider.

Jeff had a group of his own school horses, including two gorgeous Lipizzaners from Austria. Primo, one of the horses I trained, later became one of Jeff's favorite school mounts. He was well-liked among the students. Because of his thoroughbred breeding he was always energetic, unlike some of the other school horses. He had done well in dressage competitions, but never completely forgot his difficult start. Primo was always nervous outdoors with its unpredictable happenings. Schoolwork indoors had a calming effect, and the students often went on quiet hacks through the woods near the school, and Primo was well-behaved and felt confidence while working with other horses.

Primo had been on the trip to El Rocio and several fiestas. One of the fortunate features for horses is that training always gave them a better opportunity to find a caring home. At this point Jeff was able to help me with his expansive background to gain perspective about the best situation for Primo. This was the beginning of several wonderful horses and coaches who would become part of my life. Jeff also became my first coach who gave me a solid equestrian beginning with sound skills that allowed me to continually progress. With any art form it's important not to acquire incorrect habits that become increasingly difficult to change.

Jeff was an extremely positive motivator and besides consistently correcting mistakes, quickly told his students when it was "well done." These "well done" comments were given not to ingratiate himself with his students but to sincerely signify their hard work and success to obtain a difficult skill. Jeff's commitment to excellence was a reminder of the importance of positively helping people to progress in their endeavors; even small steps also give corrections for improvement.

Besides the riding classes that were held at the Sevilla Jockey Club, Jeff was always looking for ways to motivate his students. He met several of the members of the Rota Saddle Club and soon a plan to have a horse show between his riding classes and the riders from the navy base was completed. The event was highlighted in the local military newspaper, *The Jack Tar*. Magnus (1979) stated that "The Rota Saddle Club held a horse show Sunday, January 23, despite gale force winds and heavy rains. Spanish riders came from *Sevilla* to compete in the show, and took home several trophies and ribbons" (p. 8). (*Spanish for Seville)

Since the event was to promote both the Spanish and American riding clubs, several riders who didn't own their own horse were able to ride the horses from the base stable. The horse show included all ages and also family members competing in English, Western, equitation, and jumping events. Aside from weather, it was a fun event that created new friendships.

CHAPTER 4

Famous Caballos Andaluces

The famous Andalucian horses performing the traditional entry salute.

Jeff assured me that I was ready for more experiences and that he had taught me the important basics and it was time to move on to other equestrian challenges.

The riding club on the naval station and Jeff had helped start small competitions between his Seville students. Since he said that it wouldn't be impartial to judge the event, he suggested I try the Domecq School. Jeff knew about a highly accomplished rider from Portugal who was in charge of the school training program. He thought that he might be willing to collaborate judging one of the small shows, and so we were finally introduced to the Portuguese rider who was the head trainer for the famous Domecq horses. He had recently escaped from his own country because of the Portuguese communist overthrow. Portugal wasn't safe for many Portuguese and in addition, many fine horses were being sold for meat, so Francisco Cancella pursued his love of horses working with the fantastic Domecq Andalusian stallions. Not only did his resume contain the "love for dancing with horses" but a long list of famous classical coaches who I eventually would meet.

Resulting from the competitions, many interested riders took lessons from Francisco, as promoted by Jeff. I was fortunate to take some of those lessons on the beautiful Andalusian stallions of the school. The school was in an extremely large tent on the fairgrounds in Jerez that now boasts a large building modeled after the Spanish riding school of Vienna, Austria, and is situated on the grounds called Las Palacios. It was a wonderful opportunity to meet the horses who in addition became my teachers. These highly trained horses performed flying change, piaffe, passage effortlessly for a truly inexperienced rider. One of those horses was the magnificent stallion, *Jerezano*. His nickname became Jelly Roll because of the large, magnificent stallion crest on his neck. When he was working, his neck formed a beautiful and magnificent curved line. It was only when he totally relaxed his muscle that his neck appeared flaccid, giving him the affectionate name of Jelly Roll.

Cómo Bailem los Caballos Andalućes

It was Jerezano also called Jelly Roll who opened up the world of "classical dressage" and changed my life. He taught me that it was not enough to sit quietly on horseback but to then be able to ride and move by sensitive feeling. After one learns the mechanics, riding is learned through a great four-legged teacher. That is why Podhajsky (1968) said, "My horses not only taught me riding but they also made me understand many a wisdom of life besides " (p. 202). Jelly Roll was one of my teachers and was one of many horses who helped me from then on.

Besides the horses, I was lucky to also have human teachers who explained in words what the horse showed me by feel. Riding the fantastic horses they trained was an incredible experience. Francisco-trained horses were effortless to ride. Jelly Roll was ridden by a lot of riders, some very poorly and in an insensitive manner. Jelly Roll's best work was created by Francisco. I will remember that ride with Jelly Roll as long as I live.

It was also in this tent where I was to see the Olympic gold-medal rider, the late Reiner Klimke. He had made a trip to Spain and at Domecq's request came to the school to ride. The only people in the gallery were the Spanish grooms, riders, and a few of their friends. I considered myself incredibly fortunate to witness this ride. It is even more apparent now how beautiful and effortlessly he rode the school stallions, and without the obvious aids use by many who rode in the school.

It was clear that Klimke enjoyed himself getting tempi changes from horses that had been ridden by Francisco, the head trainer. Expert riders do hardly noticeable motions in their rider aids because they're able to perform by feel. Often, I watched Francisco ride a horse that I was going to ride. Try as I could, it was impossible to see his quiet cues. Simplicity is the tool of the artist.

Klimke in Olympic warm-up arena

During the California Olympics there was another fantastic opportunity presented because not only did I watch Klimke's winning gold-medal ride on Ahlerich, but more significant was watching his warm-up. He practiced the same quiet technique of asking the horse for a short practice and immediately stopping as soon as Ahlerich performed. The captivating competing ride in the arena was exciting for the audience, because he rode a brilliant transition to the canter that caused the whole audience to gasp, because they thought an error had occurred.

The warm-up technique was another example of the brilliant training that I have watched expert trainers perform, including the late Templemann. It so happened we were in Northern Germany. We found his beautiful farm where he was training the striking Japanese horse and entry in the coming California Olympics. We were surprised to see this same horse again ridden by the Japanese team in the warm-up arena. There were no fewer than half a dozen helpers running around the horse polishing everything in sight. In comparison to Klimke who eventually we were to see had one assistant, this was a hilarious sight.

During our visit to northern Germany, we were able to see Templemann ride this beautiful horse on three consecutive days. Each day, one of his competent students warmed up the horse with quiet work at the walk, trot, and canter. Templemann then mounted the horse to continue the lesson. Surprisingly, the lesson was really short and specific, especially compared to what is considered by many riders as the normal warm-up time. Each of the days he focused on a skill such as piaffe, the in-place trot. As soon as the horse performed, he immediately walked, giving the horse a free rein. These short lessons were no more than twenty minutes. There was an opportunity to ask the master about this short session technique that seemed in contrast to what most trainers performed with horses. His answer was simple: "It's important to stop the exercise with the horse's best work because that's what they'll remember."

Most of the energy in the California Olympic warm-up arena was hectic as it appeared most riders kept the horses practicing over and over the same exercise. It was different to now see the Japanese entry preparing and how different it was compared to watching Templemann working with the same horse in Germany. The other noticeable difference was Klimke and Ahlerich.

I was to have another new friend enter my life who would be trained and compete at higher levels. Interestingly the competition focus was becoming less, and the training became the goal.

CHAPTER 5

Primoroso

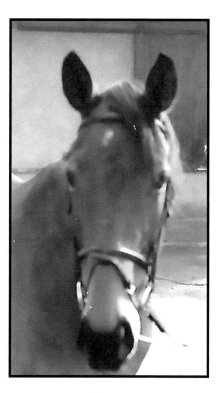

Primoroso

The Spanish weren't the only ones who kept horses in poor surroundings. I was soon to meet the American owners of Primoroso, who obviously by his surroundings weren't too enlightened about horse care. When I saw Primo for the first time he was a beautiful healthy horse with a lot of thoroughbred in him. He was pawing through what was the remainder of the lawn that surrounded a rundown bungalow that the couple rented during their tour of duty with the navy. They explained that they brought Primo home from the navy's stables, to stay in their backyard and eat grass. The stables by the way charged forty dollars a month for full care. This included grooming by the Spanish caretakers. It was obvious by the lack of grass that they couldn't or wouldn't pay the money for his board.

It was summer vacation time, time to go back to Long Island and visit the famous "Texas Ranch." Since teachers aren't paid for the summer, I needed to be cautious with my bank account, otherwise I might have paid the two thousand dollars they unreasonably asked for Primo. Two thousand was the magic number that all horse traders/sellers asked in the American market in Spain. The reasonable price was more about eight hundred for a nice horse around seven years old.

Returning a few days before I was supposed to fly home to offer them fifteen hundred dollars, Primo was standing stiff legged, eyes sunken, his glossy coat now dull and a plastic shower curtain on his back. There was no one to be found. The Spanish neighbors didn't know when they would be back and hadn't seen them for days. I left that afternoon for the States and carried a heavy heart.

Upon my return I found out that a miracle had happened: a group from the rodeo club had heard about Primo's fate, found a vet, and paid for the medication to pull him through. Now that Primo was near death's door and the couple was being sent back to the States, they gave a power of attorney to fellow sailors to sell Primo for whatever they could get.

Primo became the first horse that I bought and trained myself. I had decided to take riding lessons and learn to ride correctly. That is how I originally found "Jeff" as he was called by his friends. Mr. Jefferies was the quintessential Englishman who besides teaching history and equitation for the college in Seville also had established a school of equitation that held riding classes at the famous exclusive Pineda Jockey Club in Seville. Riding lessons on the few rainy days were unforgettable, because it was the only time that the jockeys would bring their mounts into the covered riding school to exercise. The few times it rained, it was a downpour. Jeff's school horses were very well-trained. Among them were two Lipizzaner stallions that were from Vienna. Students rode these two mounts when they had worked diligently at the basic riding skills. When the jockeys' horses got rambunctious, Jeff would order his students to halt. It was unbelievable that no horse moved until Jeff would call "walk on." We were lucky that there were few rainy days in Seville, Spain. Jeff's classes were the traditional methods used in England and riders worked diligently on basic skills, and so the beginning of a serious hobby began with a correct foundation.

CHAPTER 6

Horses and Airplanes

First solo flight at the Rota Navy Flying Club

Things have a way of changing our lives. Whether it's coincidence or a preordained life schedule is yet to be decided, but there are daily happenings that seem to be more than chance. It may be because we create a series of decisions that set certain events in motion but looking back given the perspective of time those events seem prearranged. It's amazing how chance may throw us opportunity.

The following coincidence really seems more than happenings that could have been prearranged. While attending a horse show in Portugal, the group I was with had a family commitment so I was at the hotel and eating dinner alone. When two Americans sitting nearby had some trouble understanding what the waiter was saying I volunteered to help. It was easily solved and the conversation turned to what three Americans were doing in an out-of-the-way Portuguese hotel. My explanation was that I was involved with a local horse competition. This turned out to be an incredibly strange coincidence of horses and aviation that were to become entwined in my life.

The two Americans were flying their small plane around the world making stops at various airports. Having made the most hazardous trip across the Atlantic, their next stop was Lisbon. Since it was fun for them to encounter someone who spoke their language, I was curious about their trip because I knew nothing about or anyone involved with aviation.

Their story was that the two of them were flight instructors who had decided to embark on this adventurous trip flying a small plane. The coincidence that landed them at this small hotel was the same reason that I was there. This hotel was not only located within walking distance of the horse competition, but also the airport where their plane was located.

Since they were flying at sunrise the next morning they followed the eight-hour rule I was soon to learn: Eight hours between the bottle and the throttle. In accord, we had the traditional Portuguese coffee rather than the exceptional local brandy, and I soon learned a great deal about flying small planes. I was interested about how difficult it would be to learn to fly. Since they were both flight instructors it was soon discovered that it wasn't an impossible task. Never thinking that my skills were in a technical area it seemed from the little I knew about getting a pilot license that this wouldn't be possible.

The two instructors assured me that this was easy because they knew that the Rota Naval Station had a flying club similar to the saddle club, so they would have classes called ground school. They also explained that flight schools have a flight called a demo flight. This demo flight normally costs what the plane rental would charge for the flight. On this flight an instructor takes the potential student on a short flight of the area explaining and demonstrating the type of lessons that would be taught. What they had explained was an interesting idea to explore. Since the Rota Naval Station had many clubs that supported various interests, it wasn't a surprise that one of the clubs was teaching flying because the station had a huge airport. The runway was so long that it was also designated an alternative landing site for spacecraft.

The weekend horse show was a success and the horses of Escola Portuguesa de Arte Equestre, directed by José Athayde, from Alter do Choa presented themselves beautifully. This was an opportunity to be a part of the riders from the famous school and fortunately I captured several photos of their honoring event. The summer had been an interesting compilation of riding at one of the famous centers in England and then also studying at the Portuguese school under the direction of José Athayde and riding the fantastically trained horses of Alter. Francisco and José performed a beautiful *Pas de Deux*. Besides the talented Alter stallions, the two riders coordinated the movements that use dancer's terms such as pirouette.

The summer came to a close, and it was again time to begin another school year. Since I decided to drive down to the flight line, it was a good opportunity to follow-up on what the two instructors said and ask about what it would take to learn to fly. The club office was located at the side of the taxiway by the main navy airport where several club planes were parked. Walking into the narrow metal building the first person seated at the front desk was the secretary. She answered the question that the club did offer flight instruction and could also schedule a demo flight. She directed my attention to the dimly lighted narrow end of the long building where there was another desk. The secretary called to the person seated at the desk telling him he had another request for a demo flight. The figure sitting at the desk got up and walked toward the secretary and me. The secretary introduced me to the chief flight instructor as another teacher who wanted to learn to fly; apparently five other teacher colleagues were also learning to fly. This coincidence, not presently obvious to me, would add aviation to my interests and bring me into a wonderful new future for my life, because the secretary just introduced me to Ernie.

CHAPTER 7

Petrushka

Petrushka was named after the Stravinsky ballet

Everything was quiet until the Spanish racehorses moved into the empty stalls on the other side. It seems that racing on the beach was a summer sport, so when it was too hot in Seville at the racetrack, the owners brought their horses to the beach for a vacation. Petreta, as she was known, was among the vacationing horses. I was introduced to her because she was the favorite of an American jockey from California, serving his time with the navy. He was exercising the racehorses so he could have some contact with his real interest.

The Spanish were overjoyed to have a professional working for barely anything. He would even wash them and rub their legs after the workouts on the beach. Everyone was happy, even the horses, because they liked getting the sweat, sand, and salt taken off them before being put into their stalls. Things quickly deteriorated when the Spaniards wanted to get more real work out of Mike instead of all the pampering. Mike was soon disillusioned with the Spanish racing scene when they wouldn't cool the horses down after work and they ponied young green horses down a dangerous and heavily traveled road because it was the shortest way to get to the beach to practice beach racing.

Since we were almost neighbors with my horse being stabled on the other side of six boxes where their horses were stalled, we saw Mike and his wife Jay often. One evening they both were especially upset when I arrived at the stables. The racing group had just returned from the practice on the beach. Petreta was one of these, just barely a two-year-old thoroughbred. She was being ponied along with an older horse for her first racing lessons on the beach.

It seems on the way back from the beach, she was one of the young horses frightened when chased by a dog and slipped, falling on the gravelly road. They didn't want to listen to Mike about the safe methods for training the youngsters; they only wanted it fast. When I came upon Mike and Jay they were very upset, then I saw they were with Petreta in her dirty stall where the owners had dumped her after the accident. Mike and Jay were worried because they knew it needed to be stitched. Mike did the best he could by disinfecting the gaping wound and cleaning the stall. They couldn't do anymore since it wasn't their horse. Mike cleaned it every day, but the owner's policy of saving straw for bedding wasn't helping keep the wound clean. We all were on shaky ground if someone came while doing this temporary care. Actually, there was little fear of this since they totally ignored the horses. Mike now had been dismissed and not paid by this shocking pair; we were soon to find out why.

Heavens, it's hard to understand why these people get involved with horses; they should have some kind of machine to abuse. It was three agonizing days until we were able to get an offer and pay the money for her purchase. We handed them the cash. It was here that Petreta's luck suddenly changed. Since the news that the two partners had a big fight and were selling all the horses except the top winning stallion, a window of opportunity was available. They were asking nine hundred pesetas for Petreta with her thoroughbred papers; they were hungry for the cash immediately.

Most vets connected with the military served in the capacity of a food inspector for the naval station, but since they are trained as veterinarians, they gladly accepted the extra tasks of doing routine procedures for the pets of the naval personnel. They were not able to leave the office for emergencies as we are accustomed in the States. There was the additional problem of not being able to call anyone, so I would drive to their office on the base to contact them. They were always wonderful about performing the extra effort to help an animal in distress. When I told them about this filly, he came after the office closed to the small stables located close to the naval station. It was a happy resolution and what we had done so far, even though was too late to stitch the wound, we had kept it from getting worse. We now had the additional medication to prevent infection.

Before cell phones were introduced, the telephone situation in Spain was a nightmare. Folks had to go to telephone centers or large hotels where they could make calls. When we tried to obtain a phone in a populated area where we lived it would have cost $10,000! Our friend Chuck, who had retired from the military to live in Spain, had an explanation and name for the Spanish telephone service—CTTAA— "Can't Talk to Anyone Anytime." During the time we lived in Spain during the 1970s and 1980s, this was one of the most stressful parts of the experience. During the twelve years it almost brought my heart to stop several times. Even after the dictator Franco passed, the country still wasn't making the progress as northern Europe. After we located to Germany it was a huge relief to find vets, farriers, and even horse trailers! Yes, in the future, we finally retired the 350 Ford, which now had a regular horse box installed, and we purchased a German horse trailer.

The following days found Petrushka, alias Petreta, in a nice clean stall filled with hay and a real horse vet giving her shots for the infection. She still had a noticeable scar on the fetlock joint that ran several inches as a reminder of her narrow escape. And who was this real horse vet who was later to help save her life?

CHAPTER 8

Shenandoah

Shenandoah's career as a dressage horse and capturing the lawless

When a fellow teacher suddenly returned to the States, I became the owner of Shenandoah. The first time I rode Shenandoah it was discovered that she could run just as fast backward as she could forward.

My friend had boarded Shenandoah at the navy club near the school and I had my horses at a small stable I rented from Señor Osborne, owners of the famous Jerez Sherry. The stables had been part of the Osborne summer home near Vista Hermosa.

We started to leave Shenandoah's usual turf and to ride the short distance to her new home when she decided she wasn't leaving her home. She suddenly started to cover ground in the wrong direction. Shenandoah's previous owner didn't understand teaching basic use of the rider aids; one of those aids is to move forward. It seems Shenandoah was certainly spoiled. We began to run in reverse to her barn, so I asked a friend for the loan of a crop and proceeded to the same spot of the disobedience. As we arrived, Shenandoah started to put it into reverse. This time I gently tapped with the crop once to signal walk forward. She immediately came to a shocked halt. No one has ever asked her to leave her barn. Two more tries and two light taps later. Shenandoah was walking ladylike to her new home. Shenandoah was to place in many dressage competitions in Spain, and eventually win at Seville.

Shenandoah was a beautiful example of an Andulsian that was purchased by my friend from the local horse market. She had a wonderful temperament exemplified by several stories in this book. The Andulsian is easier in temperament than the thoroughbred primarily bred for racing. This was the basic character difference between Shenandoah and Primo. No doubt there is beginning training that for horses becomes difficult to change. This is part of the reason why the stallions trained by Francisco were so easily ridden compared to the difficult stallion belonging to the English lady.

Shenandoah demonstrated this common trait of running backward because of her original training. Horses already have this instinct for protection, so it's important that they don't practice this tendency. Later I was to see and try to solve this basic training error; it was so simple when done correctly from the beginning.

CHAPTER 9

The Panels Became Lost

Xierxo performing levade

Every culture has its way of dodging difficulties. The Spanish language is wonderfully adept at helping with the problem of responsibility or fault. In English there is no way around it; when keys are lost one will eventually have to say I lost the keys. Consider the Spanish translation, the keys became lost. They just grow little legs and walk themselves away. Everyone is saved the pain of owning up to anything because things just do things or become things all by themselves. Recently, this deception has now become part of the English language.

Let's consider the 300-pound panels to partition a horse container to fly three horses from Madrid to America. The horses are loaded into a truck early Saturday morning and arrive at the airport in time for their flight at one o'clock. Their papers are only good for five days and this is the last day before they expire. My Portuguese horse, Xierxo, is moments away from his final freedom of a country that is quarantined to all countries except the States. Once Xierxo gets on the plane he will be free. I've waited and planned, cried and hoped for several years to find a way to get him out to be with me.

Saturday wears on and I think the whole day it will be hours and then he will be safe in quarantine in the States. I think of all the wonderful times we will have when he finishes the quarantine time in the States. I think about how we will start training again and how it will be to ride him every day the way we did.

The telephone rings, and I leap to answer it before it finishes the first ring. It is the American agent telling me in a voice that conveys that he doesn't quite believe what he is telling me. He stammers, trying to think how to explain that he has just received a call saying the horses are still in Madrid. After my long silence he continues. I don't understand, but they tell me they can't find the panels to separate the three horses in the large container so they didn't make the flight. He continues that he knows the panels were installed in the container when it was sent on the flight to Spain, and that they are almost impossible to move. I told the agent I knew what happened to the panels. He wondered if I had spoken to someone in Spain about the episode. I told the agent simply in a few words: The panels became lost!

Before we bought a conversion box that carries horses in the back of a pickup truck, designed with a loading ramp, I had large, heavy, thick wooden panels made for the back of the Ford 350 pickup. It normally had a camper loaded on the back, but in a pinch if I had to move Shenandoah, my Andalusian mare, I could safely transport her for short distances by installing high, heavy panels around the truck. It was a way to get around the ludicrous trailer rules and exorbitant cost of trucking in Spain. Many of the competitions were in Jerez, which was only seven miles away.

One weekend before a competition I went to have some friends help put these panels in place. They were always sitting by a covered shed built for our hay storage. They were nowhere to be seen. I don't know why it occurred to me but I remembered hearing loud hammering at the nearby house owned by a local. Wood is extremely expensive in Spain and for some reason; I sensed that those wood panels were near.

If they hadn't been painted, I knew that I would recognize them by the stamps on the wood. The wood had been purchased from the American craft shop at the base hobby shop. As we approached the wooded area, we could see beyond a small rabbit hutch in progress, being built with several large pieces of nice, new wood. We watched until the locals left to do something and approached the project for a better look. Stamped on the side of the new hutch were the words, "Special Services Craft Shop" and the identifying serial number. We left back through the trees the way we came. My friends were outraged and asked me what I was going to do. I thought to myself, what could I do, the panels became lost. (Actually, Ernie talked me out of going and demanding our wood back!)

CHAPTER 10

Shenandoah – Orthopedic Surgeon Turned Vet

Senandoah wins at Seville dressage competition

Getting a veterinarian was always a crisis. First of all, no one had phones; and second, horse vets as we know them in the States were unknown to small Spanish villages. Most of the vets in the area handled cows, and the techniques used on horses left much to be desired.

Shenandoah had picked a Sunday afternoon to cut her knee open. It was large enough to need stitches, and since it ran across the knee it wasn't going to stay closed with a bandage. There was no way on a Sunday afternoon in Spain I would find even one of the local vets. I knew that one of the American doctors might be able to help because I had coached his daughter who was part of the riding club on base. They lived nearby, so I gathered up my courage and knocked on their door. He was just on his way out, but when I told him what had happened, he insisted he didn't mind at all and met me at the stable.

It was a nasty cut and would have never healed properly without the stitching. He began to stitch Shenandoah, and as we chatted, he told me he had wanted to be a vet, but somehow his path turned to working with people. He was always helping to patch up some animal in need and loves the opportunity as he was always helping his daughter with her horses.

I later found out that "Bill" was loved by his two-legged patients just as much as the four-legged kind. He was responsible for dispensing a human caring type of medicine that was not often found these days. He still had a strong desire to not only heal the injury, but to heal the soul. People like Bill and many others I would meet through my four-legged friends spread good feelings wherever they go. They attract others who are like them, to continue living for what they do and not what they get. I was later to be befriended by one of Bill's circles of goodness.

Somewhere at a naval hospital is an excellent orthopedic surgeon who would have made one heck of a good vet.

CHAPTER 11

No Good Deed Goes Unpunished

Traditional Spanish Feria outfit

Many times, people help as exemplified by several stories. However, occasionally there are those unhappy contacts. Always looking for the next place to stable horses, we moved to the stables located on the Rota Naval Station. These moves regrettably were always temporary. The club was run by the military organization that provides activities for the military, their families, and those connected with Department of Defense positions. There were two clubs known as the Saddle Club, focused on English style equitation, and the Rodeo Club, promoting Western cowboy events.

Several of the members of the Saddle Club had seven box-stalls located at the back of the main barn. These stalls had to be cleaned and maintained by their owners. The other horses that were rentals and other horse owners were kept in a standing cement stall…no bedding and were turned out evenings in a wide expanse of many acres of what was totally wild, never cultivated, or supervised. This area was called the "Campo." It was directly behind the airfield and next to another club skeet range. During the day when the Campo gate was opened, the horses automatically came to the main barn to get grain. People who wanted to rent a horse or had their own boarded horse could ride on rough trails that wandered through the Campo.

The members of the Saddle Club enthusiastically ran all kinds of events and even had a competition in which the members of the Spanish College in Seville participated. Besides the local fiestas that featured horses, music, and dancing, there was also the yearly club ride across an area called the *Marismas* to the famous town of El Rocio.

Trail ride across the Coto Donana National Park to the famous fiesta El Rocio

The club planned a ride across the beautiful area named Coto Donana National Park to the famous fiesta El Rocio. We were given access to this beautiful, protected place through the help of a famous sherry owner because of his contact with several American club members. The trip left from the town of Sanlucar. After walking the horses a short distance along the shore, the riders all grouped for the short ferry ride across the Guadalquivir River. The small, flat ferry allowed the horses to walk onto the barge to complete the trip to the opposite side and the edge of the park. We then rode through this totally uninhabited area in the direction of the fiesta town of El Rocio. The riders as they traveled the route became aware that it would have been easy to become lost if we didn't have Chuck, a club member who knew the route.

The area was amazing combinations of desert appearing with sections of scrubby trees. The amazing animals not native to this area were the camels. Apparently, a movie group had turned their camels free after the filming and they found the habitat to their liking. The camels never came close to our group but of concern were the more adventurous and potentially dangerous wild pigs that approached the group when we stopped to rest and eat meals.

The trip was long hours on horseback but a unique experience to see firsthand and participate in a one-of-a-kind trail ride through an area that dated back to the fourteenth century royal hunting ground. In

1969 the 196 square miles was designated a national park. At the end of the ride was the town of El Rocio where many people from miles around make the traditional trip to celebrate the thirteenth-century unearthing of the discovery of a statue of the Virgin Mary in a trunk of a tree. A chapel was built on the site and the renowned celebration focuses on several days of processions and parades honoring the Virgin del Rocio. This fiesta in southern Spain is considered one of the most important celebrations in the area called Andalucía, Spain (Williams,1996).

During this time the Saddle Club made this traditional trip. El Rocio had few buildings in the sandy surroundings with unpaved roads; almost appearing as a Wild West movie set. The few existing houses had porches with a rail to tie horses. The dirt roads were large and allowed for the easy riding of horses. The club group had rented one of the few buildings for the duration of the fiesta. Various members drove vehicles on the northern roads—Seville to Huelva road—that allowed them to transport the necessary food and important Spanish wines. The days were filled with gaily dressed participants in the traditional brightly colored flamenco dresses, and a short jacket with leather chaps were the outfits of the riders.

Music was provided by all the talented guitar players who strummed the traditional melodies. They accompanied the dancing that wasn't limited to the highly trained artful flamenco dancers, but the dance that everyone learned new steps to that were added each year that was performed to the songs and clapping of *Sevillianas*. It was infectious in the beat, which encouraged everyone to participate either by dancing or clapping. It was a simple four- to seven-part series of steps that were performed with partners. Each year new songs and steps are added but following the format. Unlike the more difficult flamenco, *Sevilliana* steps are easily learned by everyone. It was amazing that the Andulsian Spanish never needed even a guitar to begin the rhythmic clapping and for folks to begin dancing the Sevillanas steps. Ernie didn't feel so competent with the dancing part, so gentlemen would approach him and ask permission to dance with me. They would hand him a glass of sherry, escort me for a dance, and gallantly return me to Ernie. These strong traditions are retained and taught to the next generation. It was one of the happiest memories of Spain; wonderfully these durable customs still remain to be passed on each year.

A humorous occurrence happened on the trip back over the unmarked trail to meet the ferry. Our small group carefully followed our guide because it would be easy to become lost. We arrived at the ferry landing and were preparing to load the horses when a riderless horse suddenly arrived to join the boarding group. At first there was concern that something had happened to the sherry owner when his horse was recognized. As this turned out that he had enjoyed too much of his company's product, and he was quickly found.

Life at the club was fun and several friends enjoyed learning about some of the horse training techniques I had learned during the vacation time in Portugal. Gladly sharing the systematic, safe, easy procedure with several of my new friends, they were overjoyed to find out how much easier their horses became. We were even able to save the life of one of the Rodeo Club's bronco horses from being euthanized because he wouldn't buck anymore and had learned to defend himself by running to the nearest fence and throwing himself at the object.

Diablo means devil in Spanish. He was an attractive horse acquired by the Rodeo Club from a local horse market. "A young woman who ran the office for the base stables purchased him to save his life, rightly was afraid to ride him" (Dammier, 2019, p. 102). Since he wasn't dangerous on the ground, the problem was to see if he could be retrained. She came to me to see if I thought the classical longe lessons would work for him. The techniques I had learned in Portugal were successful and since they had been given to me without cost, I felt I needed to pass them on with the same kindness; I had no intentions of beginning a horse training business. Little did I know that I was stepping on someone else's established part-time business.

Life went on contentedly, teaching school about five minutes away, flying lessons, and riding horses. Unless one has run into pure evil, there isn't the experience that warns anyone. Suddenly one day the school counselor came to my classroom to tell me the base stable had called and one of my horses, Petrushka, was down in her stall thrashing. The counselor, who was a friend, stepped into my classroom, which ran by itself. The next period the class would be filled with volunteer tutors for the Metra reading program that had trained volunteers and already had a schedule. No one would even know I was gone.

Unexplainably, this scenario of Petrushka being okay and then suddenly repeating the same distressing behavior happened several times. Neither the naval station veterinarian nor my horse vet from Jerez was able to explain the strange symptoms. We looked at everything in her stall, checked what she was eating, and since she didn't get turned out on the Campo at night, this was eliminated. This went on for several weeks and the vets couldn't think of a reason. At first, they thought it was colic but it seemed to reoccur on a suspiciously regular basis. It wasn't the colic that is often serious with horses…but what could she be eating?

As a friendly young thoroughbred, she had a tendency to test everything with her mouth. It appeared to the vets that she was eating something noxious and then having enough time to recover. But what was it? Blood testing wasn't sophisticated enough to send a sample out and discover what was in her system. Finally, one episode was awfully serious; she was down thrashing in pain and wasn't getting up. I went to the office of the base vet because there was no way to easily contact the other horse vet, and I thought I would have to euthanize her out of kindness. He seriously said that even though he had done his preliminary vet work with horses, he didn't know what he could do except put her out of pain. He came armed with morphine and heavily sedated her. She now was peacefully sleeping.

I always believed in the wonderful story of Sleeping Beauty and how the horrible evil fairy arranged the poison spindle to kill the princess, but then came the good fairy who couldn't change the evil spell but could intervene with a spell to soften the wickedness. Remember, the princess didn't die but merely slept. And this is what happened to Petrushka. My wonderful vet tried a last attempt to save her by keeping her partially asleep for three days. He came every several hours and administered the morphine to keep her calm, sedated, and pain free.

In an article published in the Jack Tar, *The Vet sees them all* (1982), "Care is provided to rental horses, as well as those privately owned. According to Dr. Postlewaite he sees about 350 pets a month including horses. During a recent dinner theater he was called for an emergency at the stable to tend a sick horse. In addition to missing the show, he also missed a lot of sleep, staying up most of the night."

The third day came and he said, "We're going to let her come out of the morphine and see what happens." I'm sure he still remembers this heroic try to save a horse. We stayed with her while she woke up and picked up her head and moved herself with legs still under her. I'm sure we all weren't breathing as we watched Petrushka. She sat doggie-style up on her chest looking at us as if to say, "What's going on?" Suddenly she positioned her legs and pushed herself up. She stood for a few seconds and immediately went to her water bucket and took a long drink. Our vet took out his stethoscope and listened to her vitals and quietly said that everything looked good. He set these items on a ledge in the stall and we all stood around watching her and nervously but happily talking about what a strange occurrence we had witnessed. He really didn't have any reason for what had transpired but that allowing her to be pain free helped her body to heal itself. We all stood together relieved about what we had witnessed with our attention now on the mare. We all broke out laughing as we looked at Petrushka standing there with the vet's stethoscope hanging from her mouth.

Quote from the newspaper: "We are indeed fortunate to have such a dedicated veterinary staff"(Jack Tar).

CHAPTER 12

Stranded on the Back Roads of Sevilla

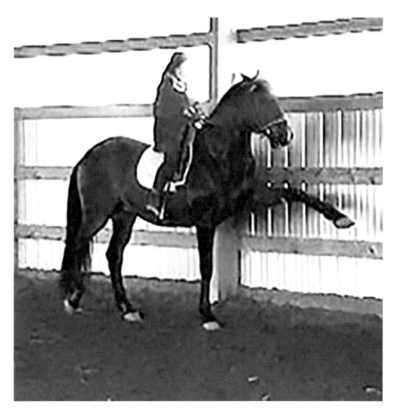

Xierxo Spainish Walk

A small-plane pilot is always looking for a place to land in case of an engine failure, not that they fail that often, but it's a training safety procedure. Traveling in Spain is similar to being a bush pilot. You're always thinking where would be the next place that I could find someone to fix our American Ford truck, which was by now so full of bogus parts it was anything but American.

As usual, the horse trips always began in the middle of the night. The roads were so difficult and the weather equally unpredictable that made horse transportation a logistical feat. This particular trip started at 0-dark-thirty and we had passed through *Sevilla* (the Spanish word for the town called Seville) in record-breaking time. Even the fiesta-loving *Sevillanas* who dance and drink sherry until the wee hours in the morning during the summer were home resting up for the next day's events. Passing through town at early morning in about thirty minutes was a treat to the normal hour and a half it would take during the day. We started the long drive on the road to Badajoz when a silence fell over Ernie and me. We knew, having flown over this stretch of land many times in a Cessna, that there aren't any towns to be seen before reaching Merida. In fact, this strip of land that runs along the Portuguese border is called *Extremadura*.

In the late seventies when we traveled this stretch of road on the way to the border crossing of Badajoz, from the time you left Seville until the Roman town of Merida consisted of two lanes and a series of twisting switchbacks, which made for a tedious drive. This is now changed and the last time I attended a conference in Spain I couldn't believe how modern the roads had become. The final town of Merida before we turned toward the border crossing in Badajoz was always the goal in case we needed help. I think we both held our breath during this stretch until we completed the last dangerous curve.

Flying over this section as a student private pilot headed to the commercial/military-run airport of Badajoz was just as scary. Navigation was almost impossible as I was to find out on a practice cross-country flight. Students practiced with an instructor before they fly the flight alone. In this case, it was important because performing dead reckoning, as it is named, was the means of navigation. This process has the pilot visually check a recognizable point on a map and compare it to a chart. This is difficult in this area because there are few distinguishing visual differences. Most of Spanish aeronautical operations were strictly commercial and small plane traffic was extremely rare. The other problem was that these airports, unless they had commercial or military traffic inbound, would shut their navigation systems down.

This area is still relatively desolate even though recently towns have sprung up catering to tourism. Recently checking with my computer map program, the distance from Seville to Merida is 117 miles and takes about one hour and forty-five minutes—more than double the time it would now take us.

We started down the twisting road in the pitch black both thinking, what happens if the truck breaks down here? We went along thinking with kind of a relief we weren't fighting the normal heavy traffic of trucks that use this two-lane blacktop road for the only connection to the Portuguese border. Things were going well and both horses were quiet in the back of the truck. We were both feeling more relaxed because we were more than halfway to Merida. The long climb had caused our trusty truck to slightly overheat, but everything now looked like it was going to be downhill. We were coming up on the last series of cutbacks, which would have been a straight and narrow road anywhere else.

Now the road has been straightened to alleviate the traffic coming and going from Seville to Portugal. We felt confident as we started up the last steep climb out of Seville. The very thing we hadn't thought about overheating was the thing we were going to need so desperately as we started our way down the other side. As Ernie knew we would be starting our descent, he has started to sparingly use the brakes as we swung through the sharp curves. In trying to give the horses the easiest ride as we pitched through the winding black ribbon that lay in the dark, we both strained to find any place that we could pull off the road and rest the brakes before they seized up. I held my breath and feared to blink. I, as the navigator, might miss any possible place to pull off.

Much of the traffic going back and forth on the road to Portugal consists of older trucks that can hardly pull their own weight, much less the goods they are overloaded with. Many of the trucks are running over the winding roads of Seville, Madrid, and the coast. Anyone who has driven in Spain in the past knows the roads were far from modern. They have thought of one thing that was our saving grace, which we were to discover just in time. Everything has now changed and many of these roads are totally modern. The last time we drove in Spain we could hardly find any of the remnants of the old roads we knew so well.

Both straining to see any place on the side of the road where we could stop without throwing the horses on a sharp angle, we were surprised to see a small road that paralleled and then went up a slight upgrade. It didn't take Ernie more than a second to check our emergency landing site and guide the truck and bring it to a safe halt. Everything was very quiet except for Petrushka, who started her usual commotion whenever the truck stopped. She always thought it was time to get off.

We both rested and waited until the early daybreak to resume the trip. During this time the silence was punctuated with the occasional squeals of Petrushka as she played with her traveling companion, the Arabian stallion Kaklak. Finally, we approached the border to wait for the veterinarian to certify the papers. This was always difficult to wait for hours with the horses in the heat and knowing we still had hours to go to reach the final destination in Portugal.

Today was our lucky day, because as we sat there in the shadiest spot we could find, wondering how long we would be there, a huge horse transport pulled next to our truck and called a friendly greeting. Jumping out of the truck to greet our friendly visitor, I recognized the famous Portuguese bullfighter and friend of my riding master. After we talked, he took our horse passports and waved as he headed off. Miraculously we now noticed our friend talking to the Portuguese veterinarian who normally could take up to four hours to complete this simple task, was waving in our direction during this conversation. Within fifteen minutes we were on our way after our rescuer handed us our papers. We asked him what we owed him. He laughed and said all we had to do was to pass his greetings on to our Portuguese friend. This is another example of the extreme kindness of other horse lovers.

CHAPTER 13

Another Stable

Dressage arena where Petrushka slid.

The Spanish saga had begun with a teaching assignment during the period of the Franco dictatorship, which added additional aspects of living there as a foreigner. The Rota Naval Station, where I had been assigned to teach, was located within easy access by several military controlled gates. Because of the differences with the contracts created between the United States and Spain, the major control for base entry was the Spanish military police. To enter the base you had to not only show the normal military identification, but also a Spanish identification card at the first gate.

At one point in time, life was easy because everything we were involved in was located on the base, one block from the beautiful apartment we owned overlooking the Mediterranean. The area had beautiful weather and many of the military retired to the area. This was also a favorite vacation place for many Europeans.

Later when we moved the horses to the navy base stables, everything was easier because I could have easily walked the distance. But of course, until we finally returned to the US, we were always playing stable roulette. This part of the story adds an episode of one of the stable changes and an upsetting occurrence. We had made another horse move to the lovely farm of an English woman who had a huge farm on the road to Cadiz where they raised a special breed of English cattle. She was an avid equestrian and had created a national level cross-country course. She was the grand dame of the English eventing scene and benefactress of these horse sports held in Jerez. Since the cross-country competitions were held on her large farm, in addition to the cross-country jumping course, she had also built a large competition-sized dressage arena. This arena was built with no cost spared. They had it graded, compacted, used rock dust with the special carpet barrier before the sandy loam. It was outwardly perfect.

Again, there was another ideal place to seriously train Petrushka. We spent many happy days and my coach even visited me here when he returned to Spain during the competitions. Because the English lady knew what a fantastic trainer he was from the time he was the head trainer and led the Domecq School in Jerez, she asked his opinion about the stallion's training. She had this young stallion in training and he was also turned out in a corral. This made what I did with Petrushka limited because I had to pay attention to the stallion's whereabouts. The English lady, even though she was a competent equestrian, was over her ability with the young stallion. Stallions become incredibly obedient when trained in more controlled environments such as an indoor arena and have a consistent repetitive program as I observed Francisco with all the youngsters. I experienced this with his beautifully trained stallions that I now competed with in Spain.

The English lady's stallion was becoming difficult and during one of her expert's training sessions, the stallion tossed his head and broke the trainer's glasses on his face. Had she listened to a real expert, this stallion could have been as good as the stallions Wembley and Palpite. Her other horses, mostly geldings and mares, trained for three-day events were adequately prepared and I ended up competing against her several times in dressage.

The time at this lovely farm passed quickly and I had good footing to train. One day we had unusually heavy rain. Petrushka and I began our normal training, walking around the arena. The sandy loam didn't even seem wet from the previous rain. We continued our normal routine of warming up at the trot. With Francisco's excellent guidance, she was easily ridden at all gaits. The trot is an easy two-beat gait that has equal pushing from all four legs. The canter differently has most of the force from the hind legs. We began to canter when suddenly her back legs were both under her body and she was sliding along the arena on her stomach. This was so quick that both Petrushka and I were stunned, and I couldn't understand why she had slipped…nothing was visually wet. The next seconds became critical as she was down on all four legs and she was still calm as I carefully stepped off the saddle and stood next to her on the ground. I still didn't understand what had happened when she suddenly sprang up. The problem was she couldn't get any footing with her legs, because unknown was that her hoof was sliding along a wet plastic-like mat. Poor Petrushka now used all her strength with her back legs but her legs slid forcefully out of control and hit me on the side of my face just over the eye. She now struggled up and was standing next to me with her reins still in my hands. We were both in shock as this was a total surprise.

Keeping the reins in my right hand and pressing my left to my face to suppress the bleeding, Petrushka quietly followed me as I led her down the short road to the stable to try and find the groom. I tried to hide what I knew would be a shock to him by turning sideways when he asked, "What's the matter?" He immediately took Petrushka because he assumed something had happened, so he put her in her stall. He now turned his attention to me as I covered my face with my hand and a scarf to keep him from seeing what I knew was not pleasant. The best place to take me was the twenty-minute drive to the military base hospital. We made the short drive as I talked to him to keep him calm and assure him it really wasn't as bad as it appeared. Arriving at the first checkpoint, the Spanish groom rapidly explained he was taking me to the hospital. To accentuate the seriousness of getting me to the hospital to the Spanish guard, I quickly removed the scarf momentarily from my face. The normally serious guard gasped and instantly ordered the young groom to immediately pass the checkpoint. He then immediately ran the short distance to the American guard to say he had an emergency with an American in a Spanish registered car that needed to get to the hospital. Since the formal agreement of the naval station was in control of the Spanish, we were dispatched quickly and arrived at the hospital door where they quickly got me to the emergency room. Later, I was to discover that the quickness of my arrival at the hospital was important.

At this point I was struggling to stay coherent and awake. Somehow I knew I had to be able to be in control. They wheeled me into the emergency room and the last thing I remember was looking up at a face I knew and saying, "Oh, it's you…Heidi!" I knew Heidi from the flying club because not only did she fly the club planes, but she was also the Rota Naval Station Hospital flight surgeon in charge of all the aviation medical services. Heidi said, "Don't worry; I'll make sure you're as good as new."

All I remembered was that I felt relieved and passed out. She was good on her promise and she took so much care with all the stitching needed that it was hardly noticeable. Everyone was surprised I looked so good after getting hit with a hoof…Heidi did a perfect job.

So, what had happened with the arena…why was it so slippery? In dressage groups this technique of leveling the riding surface, compacting rock dust, using a carpet-type barrier, and then sandy loam is one of the best methods of creating a surface of the correct consistency. The choice of the mixture of sandy loam is one of the best to not be slippery. The mystery is why this arena turned so extremely slick. The building materials were ideal until how they were combined was examined. The reason the surface was slick was that when the horse's hoof broke through the three to four inches of sandy loam, her hoof was now sliding along what was like a water slide at a water amusement park.

When we created our ideal outdoor arena here on the farm, the chap who created it knew exactly what was needed, because he also built roads and knew that they couldn't become slippery with rain. We safely rode during the rainy days of Washington…with standing water; it never had a hint of being slippery. The expensive arena in Spain had reversed the slippery barrier carpet and the compacted rock dust. The barrier carpet prevented the water from draining because it had been positioned on the top instead of the bottom layer.

After many weeks of recuperation time, we were finally back together riding. We now moved to Monolo's farm and were getting ready for the spring competitions; I was also getting ready to ride Monolo's stallions. I never found out what the English lady did about the botched arena job. She probably left it, because the whole thing would have had to be ripped up, since it doesn't rain in Spain. *"No Importa!"*

We did meet up later when we both had horses for the under six years old class in the Jerez National Dressage Competition. Petrushka won the competition and the English lady showed her true character by denouncing to the judging committee that Petrushka was over six years old. Besides having papers from the Madrid racetrack and having four-year-old teeth with hardly any wolf teeth, she got the certification of the event vet that she was not only under six but most likely hardly four. Needless to say, politics was more important and Petrushka was summarily eliminated.

CHAPTER 14

The Beautiful Andrade Horses

Ruska Dutch Warmblood

We arrived at the Andrade farm with Shenandoah and Petrushka to spend the summer vacation in Portugal. The beautiful farm had recently been returned to Sr. Fernando d'Andrade after the failed communist overthrow of Portugal.

Many of the American military stationed at the naval station of Rota were aware of this event because they frequented Portugal for a short weekend tourist trip over the border from Spain. The details of this communist takeover are unknown to the vast American population. Occasionally I found someone who knew about this communist occupation. While Xierxo and I performed at the Lusitano-Andalusian show, another participant asked about the breed of my horse. I told him how I had acquired Xierxo because of the communist takeover in Portugal. He was amazed that Xierxo, just as he, now a musician and horse lover, had also escaped this terrible period. This musician who recognized the beautiful Lusitano was as many a Portuguese expatriated, which is how I originally found my coach training horses in Spain.

Most people such as Ernie and I were so focused on other things than political affairs, even though we were living in Spain; we were completely unaware. This summer became an important view that we personally saw and wondered if this could happen to us.

Sr. d'Andrade had a goal to reestablish his life's work with these beautiful horses. The stable was filled with all these magnificent animals, which now included my two equally beautiful mares with their own separate quarters. This was a wonderful project of revitalizing classical breeding and training.

The summer progressed with riding horses and enjoying the wonderful farm. Ernie took some time off from instructing aviation classes and enjoyed a ride around the farm. Shenandoah was not only a winning dressage horse but was so easy going for a beginner such as Ernie. It was a perfect way to see the farm, which also had been a working farm with a huge cork tree forest.

Portugal had a huge industry producing cork and we were to learn that it takes seventy-eight years to produce a cork-yielding tree. During the communist takeover, all the cork trees had been harvested and sold, so there wasn't any economic possibility to produce cork for a long time. Not only were the cork trees ruined, but the farm's machinery was left to rust.

Since the Andrade horses were divided into small groups and secreted to various locations before the farm was taken over, there was now a happy reunion and the farm was given back to its rightful owner and the horses were gathered and brought to the farm. We were fortunate to view the beginning effort to again see the farm and horses endure and continue.

This was a difficult beginning for both the farm owner and the return from Spain of the classical trainer who would start the training. I was to arrive with my horses shortly after this project began. Not only did I ride my own horses but also several of the stallions in training. The unbelievable future was that these two stallions that I was riding here in Portugal were to end up in Spain and I was to ride them in several dressage competitions in Jerez de la Frontera, Spain.

The history of the Andrade family horses began with the brilliant Ruy d'Andrade as an agrarian, zoologist, historian, and defender of the national horse that is documented in his extensive writing, and the significance of this breed that has continued until now. His doctorate was in agronomics, which helped the modernization of the Portuguese agriculture. One of his works was *The Andalusian Horse* (1937). "In the following years he recognized traits of those horses in many Andalusian and Lusitano horses." His son Fernando became interested in breeding the Lusitano and developed the d'Andrade line of Lusitanos to become one of the two major and most famous lines of the breed. The stud had been formed in 1894 with Spanish mares. (Sorraia)

When again in 1974/75 the breed was threatened, Fernando sent many to the National Stud at Alter do Chao, another group to a friend, and still a third group were sent to Germany where he thought their chances to survive were better. History documents both locations in Portugal survived the revolution (Sorraia).

The days were filled with an idyllic schedule of riding horses. Often Sr. Andrade came to the indoor arena to watch the progress. By dressage standards, Petrushka, who was barely three years old, was naturally somewhat young to begin a serious riding program. He was very interested in how the mare had been begun in training because most of the stallions were about four to five years old. It was an interesting conversation as Francisco explained that after she recovered from her racehorse training accident that I had begun a systematic longe program without a rider to systematically teach her the rider aids without the stress of the rider. Of course, Sr. d'Andrade was an expert in classical training and this was merely his intense interest to know about how Petrushka was begun before he was now seeing her being easily ridden. Francisco had helped to begin her tranquil training when he was in Spain.

Ruska and Francisco extended trot

One of the beautiful Dutch-bred stallions who was beginning in training and gave no difficulty to a quiet rider was Ruska. The stallion was progressively learning to physically be trained to collect himself under the rider aids, which means the horse learns to softly give his head to the rider rein requests. The heavier warmbloods sometimes need the quiet finesse of the rider aids to yield to the rider command without physical force. Ruska already demonstrated the potential for an international level horse, especially with his easy-going temperament because of his beginning training.

A humorous episode occurred when a visiting "horse expert" who still self-promotes his knowledge was going to show us his expertise riding this glorious well-behaving stallion. After several minutes, we watched as Ruska peacefully went around the arena carrying the frustrated rider who attempted to collect Ruska…make him put his head down in the familiar position most are accustomed to seeing. Since the master, I thought, didn't feel comfortable in giving advice to another fellow "expert," he said little about changing his approach. Ruska, who contentedly continued around the arena with the increasingly frustrated rider wasn't responding to his expert rider aids. The frustrated rider now began to hit Ruska on the top of the head with his crop. Ruska, totally unaccustomed to behavior such as this, was nonplused and continued trotting around the arena.

Believe me, if Ruska hadn't been so quietly trained this could have erupted into getting the rider violently tossed. Ruska ignored this bad rider behavior because nothing like this had ever happened. The somewhat humiliated rider proceeded to hit Ruska harder on the head with his crop. Now the master immediately loudly called, "Don't do that." He knew that Ruska might not put up with the "expert" much longer and his training would irrevocably be ruined.

The master knew what most stupid trainers don't know: if you're abusive with an especially compliant stallion such as Ruska, you will contribute to a horse learning very quickly to use all of their normally peaceful personality and enormous strength against you. Because all the trainers who I worked with never struck their horses, they amazingly had these easy-to-handle stallions. Think about a tug of war game… what happens when one side releases? One can't apply force if it isn't supported. For the longest time I never saw one young horse doing anything disruptive. The most one of my stallions ever did was to take two extra long strides when a resident owl living in the old silo flew into the open side of our arena.

This lesson was to be practiced for the next several weeks as I, like many competent riders, may perform well but miss the finesse of the true artist. This was to be proven over and over as watching an artist's work makes it appear so effortless that it has the appearance anyone could easily perform. This is exactly what lured our expert into thinking he could effortlessly ride Ruska.

The day riding passed quickly and not one of the horses even my mares ever gave anything to be concerned about. This gave me a truly false impression for many years because all the riders I worked with all had the same quiet, direct handling of their horses. This example of the quiet training of the masters was exemplified later while visiting in the US for a short vacation and watching a dressage show at Devon, Pennsylvania.

The horse world is a small group and it's hard to travel without running into someone you know. Here at the show was one of the riders from the Domecq School in Spain who was competing with a beautiful warmblood. He was now living in Mexico and he and his wife had brought horses to this show to compete. We were amazed to recognize each other. While he practiced the difficult exercise of the trot in place, piaffe, the stallion became erratic in the steps, which must be a perfectly regular cadence. A European trainer, the late Ostergaard gave him clear instructions to quietly halt, leave quietly for a few steps of collected trot, and quietly halt. The rider repeated this exercise calmly. The master continued and directed that with totally quiet rider aids to now ask for the trot in place. It's one of the memorable events as I watched the horse now tranquilly trot easily in place performing the beautiful dance moving from each diagonal hoof beat to the opposite. I was to experience several talented trainers who I worked with use this tranquil method to teach the difficult exercise of piaffe and use this technique myself. After working with several masters I was able to recognize talented horses and while coaching their owners show them this skill.

After Ernie had to return to Spain to teach at the flying club, I had afternoons after the riding work was completed to ride around the farm with Shenandoah. She loved to swim and there was a lake on the property off a road that looped around the farm. She was an accomplished swimmer, having learned to swim nearby our stable in the Mediterranean. She could be ridden without a saddle, so this was easily accomplished without risking my leather dressage saddle. It was fun and we were on our way back to the main barn when we noticed a small building that resembled an outhouse. Since we had tried a different road back, this was new. The strange hut was old and rundown and looked unused. Shenandoah was extremely reliable in strange situations, having chased malicious kids on mopeds that chased her and thieves breaking into nearby homes. This strange shack didn't appear threatening, but as we confidently walked past, the old door suddenly sprang open.

What appeared in the open door was something from a horror film; it didn't look human. Shenandoah and I didn't wait and she took my cue to gallop home. We made it back to the barn as Sr. Andrade and my coach were coming out of his home. They looked surprised as she and I galloped up and came to a hasty halt in front of them. I stammered, "There is an old shack near the lake…there is some horrible-looking creature living in it!"

They both started laughing. "Oh, Patti, that's just our leftover resident communist…he's harmless."

CHAPTER 15

Fate Decided by a Fax

**We watch as the horse container is slid into the back of the plane. Flying
is much easier for the horses than truck transportation.**

With a little piece of paper sliding out of the fax machine I discover that I will finally be reunited with my mare Petrushka, who I have not seen for over three years. I just never gave up hope that somehow, I could work it out. People pick all kinds of impossible tasks and this seemed like one that would never work out.

When I look back at the pain when we were first separated, it seemed insurmountable. It lessened a little when Xierxo finally was delivered from the States. It's like some big black box that finally opens after prying and prodding it. When it finally unfastens, it is so unreal the reality just doesn't sink in. I still remember when I arrived at Rottingen, Germany, Gerd Reuter's beautiful stable, to see Xierxo standing in his stall as if nothing had happened in between. I know it will be just like that when I go to the barn, she will be standing in her box eating the nice green hay as if nothing happened.

Commercial transportation is at best difficult and stressful for horses. Petrushka will be put into a strange truck and not see anyone she knows. There is nothing I can do if I want to see her again. We have our own nice German-built trailer, which Xierxo has traveled in all over Germany, but I know from experience I would never be able to get her over the Spanish border, especially not considering what has happened in the last four years with the African Horse Sickness. There will be a Spanish truck driver who has crossed the border many times and knows everyone at the border crossings. My presence alone would be enough to keep us detained for days. We have lined up many times with all the truck drivers exporting everything you can put in a truck. This is too down to the wire.

It is more or less like being a woman piloting a small club plane on a practice cross-country from Spain into to Tangiers and having them refuse to talk to you on the radio…then they say go back. Thank heaven you have your instructor along and he tells them we're going to land, giving the tower all the directions. Their tone now changed and was, "Yes sir…copy that." These chaps didn't know they were talking to a retired fighter pilot. Sometimes you have to know when to leave it alone. Clint Eastwood said it famously: "You have to know your limitations." And I did.

After four years she will soon be here, and I will once again gain control over my mare Petrushka. Having always tried to protect my horses from the brutal reality that lies in the world for many animals, I am faced with the fact that if I ever want to see her again and enjoy all the fun times we had together, there would be some rough spots. She, unlike the oversensitive Xierxo, will fare much better with her easy-going manner.

CHAPTER 16

Career Choice

Career working with children, horses, and aviation

Outdoors and animals were loved and always a favorite pastime. Perhaps it was that various careers didn't seem self-evident as life choices weren't considered. Career plans presented themselves as I followed what were the traditional roles as counseled by school personnel who envisioned limited roles for girls my age. Jobs most suitable for women were those that would allow them to be future homemakers. In fact, I failed the standard career testing done at our high school because I wanted to be a number of different extremely opposite types of jobs.

Mostly thanks to my mother who always encouraged my many interests that I was able to pursue my lifelong dream of being outdoors with animals and including other careers. I was to counsel the daughter of a colleague to consider both horses and a medical degree. It took awhile and led through many countries and experiences, but many years later I am acting on my hopes and dreams, even though many would say it is too late to make career changes. Perhaps they are right, but I am going to continue no matter what.

Someone actually told me that they thought I was too old to be doing such activities such as taking flying lessons. It was almost believable for a moment. That feeling keeps me trying and keeps saying don't give up now after all you've done…at least discover how it turns out. And as it turned out, a career in aviation research was in the future.

So here I am at least three careers later. Besides the various careers of teaching children (horse trailered Petrushka to the playground so my class could see a horse) for over twenty years, there has been a variety of animals that brought a sizable investment of not only monetary resources but time. In difficult economic periods the commitment to horses becomes more complex, but the joy of knowing them is irreplaceable.

CHAPTER 17

Xierxo Tells His Story

Xierxo becomes a dressage horse

Born on a famous farm for producing top horses, the future was that I would become a bullfighting horse. Providence intervened and I became the beloved horse of the American student of a famous Portuguese classical trainer. Coincidence is hard to explain, but there were several events that aligned in this happening.

She had been studying during a summer with the master and they had traveled to several places in search of a suitable dressage mount. One of the places they visited was the Jockey Club in Lisbon and for fun they gave her what would be called a "man's horse" to try. She was to hear this phrase used many times, but later in Germany I was to be called a "lady's horse"; more about that later. This huge, strong jumper had a mind of his own and wasn't going to let this slip of a girl tell him what to do. She, however, upon picking up the reins that felt as if they were attached to a cement wall, decided that there wasn't any force that would change this horse in one ride, so lightly she took contact with the reins and immediately released the pressure and kept repeating this procedure. This surprised the horse she was riding because he was accustomed to strong hands and so that the try-out ride was somewhat successfully completed to the surprise of her teacher. He shouldn't have been surprised because that is how her coach had taught her. When she dismounted, he laughingly asked her what she thought. It was a rhetorical question of which they both knew the answer.

It was providential that we would meet when the master brought her to see me as a beautiful two-year-old. I was free running around in a partially opened indoor arena that allowed sunshine and a flock of small flying birds inside. I took to showing off leaping about at the flying birds with the sun glistening off my shining dark coat. She was head over heels in love with my beauty and I had an instant career change to a dressage horse.

A young lad did the classical longe work and got me accustomed to a saddle and rider. She was accustomed to riding young horses and so we started what became twenty-five years of being together. I never forgot about my bullfighting talent and as you will read in her other stories I could whirl in place when something worried me. I didn't buck or run or anything naughty as most horses but merely quietly whirled on the spot. My new owner was always quiet with me and sat so well that I would gently carry her during the whirl. There was only one time when we separated during the twenty-five years together and it was during a ride outdoors in the fields in Germany when she broke her rule about wearing boots and riding clothes.

Life was a blur from Portugal and then to Spain, when suddenly I was rushed to the airport and a flight to the United States. I thought my beloved mistress had abandoned me when I was shoved around by strangers and finally ended up at a place that seemed as if it was a prison. I was well fed but there were no outings and I stayed what seemed endless days in my stall. Then one day a young groom came and put a halter on me and was leading me outside. I was frightened because I didn't know what was going to happen to me. We walked outside and headed in the direction of a high chain-link fence where I noticed a couple walking toward the fence. The lad yelled something at the man and woman and they suddenly stopped short of the high fence. I couldn't recognize who they were but out of the blue I heard a voice calling my name repeatedly. Amazingly I recognized the sound of her voice—how could she be here? I picked up my head high to try and see her. At this moment, the lad who held the lead line was scared that I would run away and began to yank at the line. I heard her calm voice and a German sound that I understood; he stopped yanking the line because I now stood quietly listening to her talk to me— everything was peaceful. I was calm and knew everything would be all right. We turned and walked back to my stall and things seemed more normal; I knew it would be okay.

In what seemed a short time, I was again unceremoniously put on a truck but this time when I arrived, it was at what I recognized as an actual farm. We drove up to the building and as I was getting off the transport I heard that wonderful voice, and suddenly she was there taking charge. We had arrived at a trotter's training barn because the local, famous, nearby dressage training barn wouldn't have me because I had been at the state quarantine facility, even though I served my time and was released. It was wonderful watching all the trotters practice every day. The dedicated couple who ran this trotter barn were happy to have us and we would ride on their beautiful track as long as the trotters weren't practicing.

Things were wonderful for the summer but she soon had to return to Germany and begin the school year. I stayed at the beautiful farm and was lovingly exercised on the longe by a young woman she trained and paid so I could stay fit. Her mother who loved animals and lived nearby would visit me every few days to check on me. After the ninety days in the United States I was allowed to leave. Again, I boarded another flight and was delivered to follow her to Germany and to live at the beautiful stable of a famous German trainer, where she rode me under his instruction every day. He loved working with me because I could effortlessly perform the exercises of piaffe and passage, which were difficult for many of the German breeds. Being taller than many Lusitanos, they couldn't look down on me even though I had a different head profile: the traditional regal Baroque silhouette.

Finally, the German story came to an end and I was back on a plane headed to Washington State. This time, she was driving me in our German trailer from the German farm to the Frankfurt airport, with the quiet loading accomplished by Lufthansa. My new friend, a young Trakehner mare was traveling with me and we were soon onboard with a third horse in our travel box. Soon I found out that she was on board as a passenger because it was what is called a combi-flight. After we were at altitude I was so happy because she was allowed to enter the cargo cabin behind where she was sitting along with another passenger, who also had horses onboard. She carefully checked on us, plus the third horse in her care, to make sure we had water and hay. She knew we could easily become dehydrated on the eighteen-hour flight.

Once again, I had another pretty hectic truck ride with my new horse friend on the trip from California to Washington State during what turned out to be one of the state's serious storms. She was unable to pick me up at the airport because the German horse trailer hadn't yet arrived. It was another worrying time while she waited for me to arrive.

We had a few temporary boarding farms but finally I had a wonderful home with my own outdoor pasture shared with my favorite Trakehner mare. She had traveled with me from Germany and was only two and especially nervous about flying. I assured her I had flown several times and she shouldn't be worried. We began a friendship as pasture mates and I helped her raise three youngsters that are still on the farm.

Life was wonderful as my mistress developed her dream farm with beautiful indoor and outdoor dressage arenas. She and her husband worked hard teaching aviation courses. Everything worked around the farm so everyone would be cared for. Besides the horses born on the farm, two more German horses arrived.

When I was fifteen, I became dreadfully ill with what all of us horses worry about—colic. She rushed me, with the help of several friends, to a nearby veterinary hospital that specialized in equine surgery. She stayed and watched the operation and didn't leave until I was in satisfactory condition. She and her husband drove every evening to visit me. There were wonderful veterinary assistants that had to perform that procedure of refluxing, because we horses can't regurgitate. These assistants were so skilled at this difficult and unpleasant procedure of placing a tube down your nose that we didn't even know anything bad was happening. This single difficult task performed by these future vets was probably one of the single procedures that allowed so many of their patients to survive the recovery time. I went three almost four weeks without eating anything and she was scared I would starve. Her veterinarian explained that I was in such fine muscle and health that it would be a very long time before I would starve. She learned that horses are without food for a long, long time before it's noticed.

Things were looking up and I was going to be able to eat fresh grass, which wasn't exceedingly available in November. She and her husband cut a fresh grass that was on their farm called canary grass, which grows at the edge of wetland. Every day they filled their SUV with the sweet grass and there was enough to share with my friends. After about six weeks I was finally loaded in my German trailer and taken home. I had to take huge amounts of antibiotics that were fairly pricy since they were the same antibiotics for people…only I weighed about 1,700 pounds!

Seeing my other horses lifted my spirits and it was good to be home. After many months of getting fit and healing a very long incision on my stomach, I was able to return to light exercise, first on the longe and eventually under saddle.

We didn't return to competing, but I performed my fantastic musical routine for the Lusitano and Andalusian club where I was invited each year. She had several young warmbloods to train and it was probably best that I had semi-retired, since I was lucky to be alive. I had taught several students at the club in Barcelona, Spain to perform flying change and several more students here to do passage and piaffe, so I felt life was enjoyable. I did go to a riding clinic with one of the warmbloods and she also rode me during the clinic for a demo. It's a small world and the international judge who knew my German trainer was doing the clinic and did ride me at the walk to demonstrate an exercise to the group. After all, I was a lady's horse.

It was a wonderful life. My dear mistress is still here on the farm with the last three horses born on the farm that I helped raise. And I am here too, where she at last led me and later my favorite mare, on exactly the same day, two years apart on Three Kings Day. My other friends are also here to remain in our favorite pasture.

CHAPTER 18

Xierxo, The Rest of His Story

Xierxo

The communist takeover had not only ruined the horse industry, it had also ruined the Portuguese escudo by making it valueless. The dollar became strong in purchasing power, so through my exceptional contacts I became the owner of the two-year-old Lusitano stallion, Xierxo. He stayed with us until the end of his life on our farm. He could have gathered frequent flyer miles with all his travel time between the United States and Europe.

He was delivered to the Portuguese farm where I was studying dressage. The first time I saw him, he was running around free in a semi-opened arena chasing little birds that darted in and out of the open side. The open side allowed sunlight to enter, which attracted the birds. He leaped off the ground trying to catch the birds with his hoof as they flitted around. The sun was shining on one side and the other was rather dark. Where the two sides met in the middle, a strange dance took place with the birds and horse. His sides glistened in the sunlight and bounced off the whirling birds. I was mesmerized by the scene as I realized this beautiful horse was mine and was to be with me for twenty-five years. Xierxo was bred by a famous farm for producing bullfighting horses, noted for their athletic ability. A famous bullfighter wanted to purchase him but fate was on Xierxo's side; because of his extreme sensitive personality, it would have been a difficult life compared to becoming a dressage horse.

My talented Portuguese coach was pleased that I had acquired this horse and the serious classical training began. This work was begun on the longe whereby the horse learns to walk, trot, and canter without the rider. When the horse has this level of training the rider is added. Without exception the horses, mostly stallions, never bucked. After using this classical method for starting all my young horses, I didn't see horses purposefully buck their rider until I came to the States and helped riders with the difficulties of not allowing the horse to move athletically forward; exactly how you create bucking.

It was during the summer I purchased Xierxo that I bought Petrushka, a thoroughbred mare, off the Madrid track as a two-year old, and trained Kaklak, a perfectly formed Arab stallion in the classical Spanish style. The summer was spent training horses and getting to know Xierxo's unique ability. He had the light movements of the Lusitano breed and lightning quick reflexes of what is considered an ideal bullfighting horse. This was no surprise, because he did come from one of the largest Portuguese farms that produced these horses. He was slightly larger than many Lusitano horses but had the ability to collect himself on his hindquarters in a second. In fact, he was always collected by his build and different from my warmblood horses with longer frames and extended movements. Interestingly, these two breeds can be trained for both collection and extension. Xierxo's beginning training focused on lengthening his stride, which gave him fantastic passage and extended trot.

In his beginning training he'd be moving in a beautiful frame and suddenly see a minuscule spot on the ground and collect himself and gracefully move away from that spot. The rider would find that they had gracefully moved slightly sideways but were still going forward. He carried himself so naturally collected that he easily carried the correctly seated rider along, because it was such a smooth level motion it was almost unnoticeable, not similar to the often-frightened hectic motion of younger horses. It never was any cause for alarm because he had such wonderful control in this maneuver of the moment. The rider just had to make sure they were always paying attention and sitting deep in the saddle in order to be carried along. I became accustomed to riding him…it was like floating on a cloud.

Bullfighting bred horses have a natural ability to whirl on their hind legs and change direction in an instant. Often riders play with these natural talents and later find to their dismay that the horse uses this talent against them. I knew that if I persisted with the basics of moving forward, creating this as his habit, I'd later be able to enjoy the exercises of half-pass, extended trot, piaffe, passage, flying change, and levade.

The only concern with Xierxo was that the rider had to pay attention to their position in the saddle. Riders and trainers don't get a talented sensitive horse that can do multiple flying changes with hardly more than thinking the aid, without some difficulties resulting from that sensitivity. While competing in Barcelona, Xierxo decided there was something about one side of the dressage arena he didn't like. After he refused two changes of direction, I decided this was going to be a learning experience and try to urge him to complete as much of the test without resorting to overuse of aids. It turned out well because later after the event we were able to walk calmly around the arena, and the next day he successfully completed the test. People who had seen him the day before couldn't believe how different he was.

In his life, Xierxo did twice unseat riders: one of my coaches and me. I call it unseat because it was very quiet. It was as if someone gently pulled a chair away when you were going to sit down. Both times he did it while quietly standing at the halt. Something would get his attention and he would do the quick whirl in place. We joked that it was as if he needed glasses because small things suddenly appeared in his sight. If the rider was paying attention and sitting deeply in the saddle, it was a collected half-pirouette. When I rode Xierxo I always had riding pants and boots on so I sat deep into the saddle and correctly balanced.

One time he performed his quick unseat with me while riding outdoors on a German farm that produced sugar beets for the local breweries. Since the change in ownership of the beautiful farm caused the boarding fee to triple, it was more than the mortgage payment on our German house. This constant stress of always trying to find the next farm wouldn't end until we finally had our own perfect farm in the US. This new farm that we were boarding at didn't have much of an indoor arena. In fact, after my coach's beautiful Olympic-style indoor riding arena with perfect footing, lighting, and size, this was completely the opposite, including six supporting poles located in the middle. It was temporary until we could find another boarding place…again.

Ernie's riding days were finished when his heavy aeronautical teaching became demanding of his time. He did decide to buy a mountain bike so we could enjoy a four-mile trail on this huge German farm. It was decided that Xierxo should get more outdoor training and I shouldn't be riding alone. So almost every day after school, he left his office on the nearby military base and we enjoyed this wonderful tour. Xierxo became so accustomed to following the bike that I could drop the reins and he would follow it. One time in an open field we used as a training space, Ernie on his bike made all types of circles and changes and Xierxo followed him as if he were a cutting horse chasing a cow.

This day, however, my bag with the regular riding clothing was forgotten and I was dressed in a slippery polyester warm-up pants and jacket. My rule was that I didn't ride my horses without riding outfits, including boots, because this encouraged the rider to perch on the saddle instead of the deep classical seat. Riding an athletic horse, demands that the rider also is supplely in the saddle. I remembered saying to my husband, who always went on the outdoor excursion with his mountain bike, "We're only going for a short ride through the nearby field. It will be all right that I'm not wearing my riding stuff." We did this outdoor ride around the fields and tractor road through the forest almost every day, so it seemed safe for this one time.

It was a beautiful afternoon as the mountain bike and Xierxo headed down the lane. We reached where the lane turned to head toward the forest and I stopped. We were all standing quietly when Xierxo noticed a pile of wood nearby us that wasn't there yesterday. Since I was always aware of his reactions, I could see his head quickly turn as if he had seen a ghost. All of a sudden he did his whirl and of course with the slippery pants, in seconds I was standing on the ground. In our twenty-five years together, this was the first and last time I ever broke my rule about riding without riding clothing, especially with Xierxo.

The second instance happened with a top classical trainer, who was riding Xierxo while I was in Spain. The custom was for visiting onlookers to enter the seating area and reach over to shake the hand of the trainer in the riding arena. Xierxo was standing quietly with my coach, greeting the guests. The sitting area was elevated to the person shaking hands so the rider was at the same level. Xierxo stood quietly during several handshakes where the rider had to lean over slightly. For some reason one of these visitors got Xierxo's attention and in a flash, he made a sudden whirl exactly in place away from the extended hand. The rider was now standing on the ground looking up at the visitor and Xierxo was standing quietly next to him as if nothing had happened. This was the only time a horse had ever done this to him—Xierxo was the horse.

CHAPTER 19

Story Fax

Teufel- the wonderful gift from Inger

It is three years since I've seen Petrushka, but as I sit here I can dream of the first moment when I will see her again and we will start to work together. I have talked to all my friends who are taking care of her in my absence. I call them long distance to find out how she fared in the long trip from Spain to Germany.

The whole story is so typical of all the things that have happened in the last three years that kept us apart. After finally getting the Spanish agent to deliver her to Germany now that the border is open because of the Olympic Games, they decide to deliver her three days after I have booked a flight to take classes in Florida with a university. It is one of those things that you plan and plan for and then you finally throw your hands in the air and say it will happen if it is meant to be. It is hard to realize that there are things that are outside of one's control. I had planned everything to the last fax. And in keeping with today's technology, it was a fax that decided Petrushka's fate.

Again, the kindness of several friends made it possible and I know this responsibility to stand in for me, added extra responsibilities to their already full lives. Fortunate can't begin to describe all the wonderful people who helped. Friends come in different wrappings, but one thing they all had in common was that they loved not only horses but animals, especially dogs and cats.

My friend Inger loved and befriended many homeless cats. I had met her when four of our classrooms had been assigned to an unused German school that was near the overcrowded main school. Inger's eighty-plus-year-old mother was in charge for the care of the four-room schoolhouse. She was amazing and an example of the strong generation who survived the Second World War. Inger came by to see if her mother needed any help, not that she needed any. Since I speak fluent German, it was an opportunity to learn a historical perspective that is missing today. Inger became a dear friend, and I was gifted one of her beautiful doll-faced Persians she acquired from the pick of the litter by breeding one of her beloved Persians. She said anyone who takes all her pets with her, wouldn't turn around and sell her gift. That was true and the beautiful *Teufel* came with a cat rescued by my mother, named Snowball, in their cat carrier along with Xierxo and Fanfare. They had a comfortable flight to Los Angeles, along with the German Shepherd on board. They could share a container so they wouldn't feel alone and I could check on them for food and water. They would also hear a friendly voice. Inger was there visiting when the fax arrived at our German home. She understood the happiness I felt.

After three years of waiting, a fax rolled out telling me that Petrushka would be delivered from Spain to Germany. Great moments are often seconds of insignificant trivia.

CHAPTER 20

Shenandoah Rides Again

Shenandoah with her foal, Shembly

The first time I rode Shenandoah I discovered that she could run just as fast backward as she could forward. My horses, however, were at a nearby stable owned by the local and famous Osborne Sherry winery. The stables had been part of the summer estate near the beach overlooking the Mediterranean.

When we started to leave Shenandoah's normal turf to ride the short distance to her new home, when she decided that she wasn't leaving her stable and started to cover ground in the wrong direction running backward. Her previous owner most likely used the corrective technique of backing a disobedient horse. In my books, *Behavior Modification for Horses*, *Horse Makeovers*, and *Positive Horses,* I explain how various rider techniques may have an unfavorable outcome and how those behaviors may be changed. Rather than teaching a horse to move on clear commands, shortcuts are often used. Besides being a winning dressage horse, Shenandoah outsmarted the lawless.

At the international Jerez Dressage Competition, we decided to walk the short distance from the fairgrounds of the competition to the stabling. It was a short dirt path that ran between as a shortcut behind apartments and buildings. Many of the competitors used this shortcut, so we walked the horses among pedestrians, bikes, and occasional mopes (motorized bicycles). Everyone loved seeing the horses and riders outfitted, as the Spaniards so enjoy their costumed festivals and they were very respectful of the group. All the spring festivals/fiestas in Spain are focused on horse events. The pedestrians would sometimes stop and ask to pet the horses and ask about the competition. The many horse competitions are held right after the holy Easter celebrations/parades and are part of the lovely fiestas held by each town; Jerez de la Frontera being one of the largest. Most everyone was extremely considerate of the horses, and the motorized moped riders respectfully avoided the horses. We were quietly walking back after the day's competition when two of these mopeds maliciously tried to scare Shenandoah and then prevented her from passing along the dirt strip. Many Lusitano and Andalusian horses are especially talented athletes with great ability to balance easily on their hind legs. They effortlessly learn what the Spaniards call *"Alta Escuela,"* which are the classical airs above the ground. Physically, their shorter backs compared to the warmbloods make the exercises easier. I immediately put Shenandoah into a canter and charged at both of them. Next, I gave her the "levade" cue and she effortlessly balanced on her hind legs in the position of a warrior horse that makes the horse present the full chest, thus protecting the rider. Today, somehow Shenandoah thought she should add to her trick and began to wave her large hoofs in their faces. Before anyone had realized what was happening, these two naughty kids quickly motored away screaming at the top of their lungs while the onlookers broke into laughter and applause.

CHAPTER 21

The Wonderful Horses of Alter do Chao

José and Francisco with Alter stallions

Every time I drove into the town of Alter do Chao I had the impression of stepping back in time. Life seems to proceed at a more leisurely pace than elsewhere. The small and one of the few hotels located right in the center of town had several shops and businesses; this has now changed and there is a huge hotel complex.

The hotel was a center for midday meals for many, including many of the riders connected with the equestrian center. Meals, which were taken in a coffee room on the first floor and in an additional room on the second level were always wonderful in their home-cooked simplicity. As I took my normal English-style tea called *cha,* I was truly ready for another day with the talented teaching stallions of the Alter school and their head school master José d'Athayde.

The exercises of the Portuguese School of Equestrian Art are based on lightness and on almost indivisible aids, so that rider and horse may be seen as whole. Such is the riding that I have been practicing for the last 50 Years, that was passed to me first by my father and later by Master Nuno Oliveira, as well as by D. José d' Athayde and by Dr. Guilherme Borba – founder and first Director of The Portuguese School of Equestrian Art. (J. Filipe Figueiredo (Graciosa), Head Principal Riding Master and Director of P.S.E.A. (Portuguese School of Equestrian Art)

(Yglesias de Oliveira, Celestiino da Costa, 2012, p.62).

The grounds themselves were beautiful in the old-style building and the indoor arena with the large galley where visiting tours often came to watch the daily training. Each day's schedule was similar to many large training schools. The younger horses were started first in longeing lessons (lessons on the line to learn walk, trot, and canter commands), and then ridden by the assistants who were also the horses' handlers. The difference was that here, occasionally outside students were admitted to ride and train under the talented watchful eye of José. Now the director of Coudelaria de Alter do Chao, José brought to the school the best of the Portuguese School of Equestrian Art.

I was lucky to spend my summer vacations so occupied and it was one of the hardest things I had done, but this prepared me for many difficult future goals. Many would call the teaching system old fashioned because many of the senior masters figured if you couldn't take strong criticism then you shouldn't be there. There were many students who happily would take the place and consider themselves lucky. In a way, it was a motivation test. As a professional educator, I would be the first to agree that for certain subjects and groups of students that this type of pressured motivation would be inappropriate. At beginning level skills, a positive motivational approach might be more successful. However, this learning also demanded that the student press themselves to a more difficult level.

There are moments in our lives when we drop our normal routine responses and honestly act for what happens in what I call a transparent moment. These moments allow us to face unpleasant happenings truthfully and learn something about our inadequacies, instead of covering for mistakes or shortcomings. And so it is with learning any difficult task, whether it's flying, playing an instrument, painting, or heaven forbid learning to play tennis, the act of learning a new skill renders a person transparent. That is to say if something will be learned the learner must be vulnerable to reveal openly what they don't know rather than keeping the pretense of being able to do the tasks. The transparent moment came with learning the difficult art of dressage.

Since arriving back in the States, I have noticed that this type of formal riding school is rare. Students merely take private lessons on their horse and expect to be told how wonderful they are in front of their peers. I didn't take private lessons until much later and lessons were in a group of riders under the eyes of the head trainer who gave commands that weren't questioned but obeyed. The corrections were made to each rider, such as sit straight, quiet hands, and look forward. There wasn't any time to question because you needed every bit of your physical and mental strength to keep up with the lesson. It was similar to what would be expected in any serious music or dance class. There are beginner classes for those starting to learn.

Shortly after arriving back in the United States we went to visit a large riding center to watch a dressage clinic to see what was going on in the equestrian world. This first observation made me realize how different riding lessons were here compared to Europe. The first lesson we observed was a young woman riding her lovely, well-behaved horse, and after completing a few minutes of sitting trot actually complained that she was tired and had to stop. I couldn't believe this nor could my husband Ernie, who was often filming many of my lessons. We were both astounded when the foreign instructor acquiesced and they both took a long break. Would you mind if you were getting over $100 for the lesson? It was encouraging to hear two women who were sitting nearby, one who was the rider's normal instructor, discuss how disappointed they were and that this wasn't the approved standard for advanced riders.

The second lesson was also with this well-known European trainer who I know didn't accept this kind of behavior, because young beginning students who haven't developed the physical strength to ride a horse are taught on older school horses. The teacher has the school horse on a long line-longe line and controls the horse. After the student has progressed, and can walk, trot, and canter with the school horse, they then may advance to an easy class group lesson with disciplined school horses. The students ride in groups and learn the exercises before advancing to private lessons.

This lesson had a young teenager who was riding a beautiful horse. It was obvious after a few minutes watching that the training, at great expense, was done by someone else. This horse had the perfect gaits of a beautifully trained athlete. The horse moved with a graceful elegance and it was immediately noticeable that the rider wasn't his equal.

The German trainer was able to encourage her to be quieter in her responses to the horse, because he could see that this was a brilliant horse. We could see that this horse compared to the top performers we had seen in Europe. He gave the rider several basic commands and then asked her to halt. The instructor wanted to see the quality of her basic rider commands. It soon became obvious she assumed that her riding skill inadequacies would be obscured by owning a dazzling horse. The impatient rider half-listened to the instructor as her horse nervously responded and anxiously fretted when commanded to halt. When she finally stopped making aggressive hand motions, the horse behaved beautifully and quietly stood. Even though the instructor quietly elicited her cooperation with handling the horse, her disagreeableness was evident. The instructor told her that she owned a finely trained horse but this actually made her attitude worse. The persevering instructor whose concentration was able to have the horse perform for the rider, was able to have the horse end the lesson on a positive note, however, this result was totally lost on the rider. It was disappointing to watch a rider who had the best possibility that others wished they had to be completely ignorant about the wonderful opportunity to learn from this noble animal.

Your horse is your mirror.
— *Old* German proverb

At the end of the lessons, all the horses were being groomed in the nearby stable. We walked over to see the horses and chanced to overhear comments from the last rider as she unceremoniously shoved her horse into an empty stall, without the customary grooming. In summary, she stated she wasn't going to keep this "stupid horse" because her parents were going to buy her a new one. This rider's revelation was certainly a transparent moment to me.

Needless to say, the lessons with José were not rest sessions or doing the easiest exercise you already knew how to perform. If riders expected to be applauded for exceptional performance, the reward came from knowing how hard you worked; it was fun. Everyone riding in that hall knew that they were privileged to be there and were dedicated to the art of the stallions.

Alter do Chao was a popular tourist place. There were always visitors in the upper viewing gallery and at first this was a distraction. As an outside visiting rider, I became accustomed to riding in the hall with not only José with all the other regular assistant trainers, but also the constant stream of tourists visiting the famous horses. It was a lesson in not being preoccupied with self-image but working as hard as you could to learn something new alongside the other hard-working assistants. It was a freeing experience not being concerned with making a mistake but rather striving for a goal. It was an important lesson that will stand me well in many other difficult tasks.

The horse exercises now became much more difficult than the classes I had learned with Jeff. Significantly as a British equestrian judge, he provided an excellent course as outlined in all the British Horse Society documents that provide the student with an important foundation. The Alter horses performed all the classical movements that one equates with the famous Spanish Riding School of Vienna. It was always a joke that the Alter horses only needed Walt Disney to produce a film such as the *Miracle of the White Stallions*. This film is a beautiful tribute to the Lipizzaners.

Girded with a solid equestrian foundation, the task was to add more difficult skills on to the groundwork. Looking back, it seems significant that basic skills are important in any lesson, whether it's teaching young children to read or perform difficult equestrian exercises that are often called "high school." This means that the horse is not only going forward in their normal gaits but they also learn to perform what can be seen naturally running about and under the direction of the rider. These movements include moving sideward, and appear to be skipping, called flying change, and balancing on their hind legs called courbette capriole, and levade. The Alter horses performed these exercises effortlessly.

During one of my lessons, I was practicing a simple depart into the canter in preparation for learning flying change, the horse with very slight cue changes from one leg to the other in a sequence. These advanced horses become so in tune with their rider, and sensitive to the slightest change of the rider's position, not even seen by others, that they understand the difference between each exercise with the slightest cue. I had been given the command to canter, when my mount clearly told me it was wrong and began a beautiful passage. The passage is a slow animated trot, with a pause of high suspension when the horse holds himself in the air and repeats the floating trot step. It is an amazing feeling of floating and the wonderful stallion continued this fantastic movement around the hall with me as a mere passenger followed by Jose's crescendo calls to stop passaging and canter. The more I tried to get the stallion to canter, the more he passaged. Besides my increased awareness of my failure, I now had the whole school of assistants who halted their horses watching what they all knew could happen to them. The scene went on for what seemed an eternity to the continued calls from José. I glanced upward trying to gather my thoughts only to see a busload of tourists had arrived in the gallery as more witnesses to my transparent moment.

For all you riders who know what I should have done sooner, I calmed myself, sat quietly, and asked for the halt. My wonderful horse quietly halted softly and stood waiting. Everything in the hall paused with us for that moment and not a sound could be heard. As if someone pushed "play" the gallery visitors shuffled, the assistants began riding, and my gracious horse began to slowly walk around the hall on a free rein.

CHAPTER 22

Unicorns on the Beach

Lusitano stallion Palpite wins at Jerez dressage competition

It is a small world and just how small is discovered when you meet people and horses who you know and also who know each other. During the time I rode at the farm of Andrade there were many beautiful Portuguese stallions and many kind, horse-loving people who came to visit. One couple was an English pair who had a farm on the coast. She had several finely trained dressage horses and competed both in Portugal and Spain. When I met them at the farm and later visited them at their lovely farm on the coast I didn't ever think I'd become the recipient of a great act of kindness because of meeting them. As one brushes with the occasional evil, one more often brushes with good. This elegant couple still remains in my thoughts and appreciation.

Petrushka and I were staying in Portugal for the summer but then it was necessary to bring her back to Spain and there didn't seem any way to do this long trip again easily. These two lovely people were coming to Spain with their horses for the Spring Feria and offered to bring Petrushka with them. After offers of payment were refused, they merely said that they were coming to Jerez, Spain, and there was room in their van, so why not? There are people who just do kindnesses and never expect anything in return, unlike the "Jays" of the world. All legacies are written by daily acts.

One of the horses that I rode while staying on the Andrade farm was a well-trained, pleasant white horse that didn't have any particular talents but was an especially agreeable ride. I later found out he was part of a team of special carriage horses and was trained by my coach and spent time with the driving program of Alter do Choa.

Jerez has one of the most spectacular horse fairs that are known as Ferias. During this week-long celebration of competitions, shows, and horses parading in the streets, there are performances of carriages with every description of numbers of horses and types of carriages that may be seen at a lengthy show at the *Yeguada Militar*, Jerez. (Founded 1874 for breeding Andalusian and Arabian horses.)

The next time I met these two *Cartujano* carriage horses they weren't matched with an elaborate outfit for a carriage parade but were on the beach on the coast near Puerto de Santa Maria across from the Bay of Cadiz, where we lived. "Nearby is the *Finca San Jose del Pedroso*, the stud for the famous Terry horses, the white pure bred *Cartujanos*, which are stabled in the old bodegas of John William Burdon."

The famous horse photographer Robert Vavra was coming to shoot photos for his upcoming book about unicorns. They were going to be shooting the pictures on a small beach in Vista Hermosa. In order to assure the safety of the "unicorns," a human ring was appointed to make a living chain to contain the horses between the rock jetties and the open beach. This jetty can be seen in the background of the picture of the two horses on page sixty in the book *Unicorns I Have Known.* This barrier provided security on one side and the helpers provided a guard on the opposite side so the horses couldn't run down the open beach. The book is a wonderful addition to a horse lover's library because it may be left on a table to not only look at the beautiful photographs but read the inspirational poetry that Vavra (1983) included for each photograph. Here is one of the quotes (p. 56).

All the beasts obeyed Noah when
He admitted them into the ark.
All but the unicorn.
Confident of his own strength, he boasted "I shall swim."
Ukrainian folk tale

The impromptu audience watched while the two played and frolicked as if they were reading a script. The pair joyfully swam in the surf between adjustments of their coiffured mane and unicorn horn and seemed to unquestioningly accept this costume while they continued their surf play. The elaborate hairpieces and realistic horn were attached in an elaborate manner that was undetectable to an observer. The hair design was so perfectly done that even the horses carried them as they were part of their anatomy and the effect was dreamlike.

A large group of onlookers had respectably gathered at the top of the jetty to peer down to the pair of unicorns frolicking in the surf. Vavra continued photographing, loading a bulk loaded camera while waiting for the perfect time when the lighting would yield the ideal highlights. We watched mesmerized as the intense sunlight took on the perfect shadows and highlights of another perfect Spanish sunset that may be seen in the section Vavra entitled *Unicorns of the Sea*. Looking at several pages, the differences in the light are observable. My husband, who was standing behind the photographer's view, chatted with one of the incredulous onlookers who had recently arrived at the viewing spot. After the preliminary questions about what was going on and being told a short summary about Robert Vavra and that the photos for his new book were being taken, the observer continued to stare intently. Following a lengthy silence, he disbelievingly replied, "This is amazing…I didn't think unicorns existed anymore!" But hopefully also acts of kindness because all legacies are written by daily acts.

CHAPTER 23

Mentor and Mentoring

Stallion performance

The head of the *Real Escuela Andaluza del Arte Ecuestre* was a classically trained equestrian with much experience working with highly trained horses. Francisco Cancella was one of many of the Portuguese who left Portugal during the communist takeover. His family and friends' safety were at risk. Being schooled in the art of masters such as Borba, Oliveira, he had the position of head trainer at the national school of Jerez and was an excellent trainer who was methodical and patient.

After the excellent beginning with Mr. Jefferies, Jeff as he was affectionately called, sent me off to find my next teacher, as a principled educator does with their students. It is only the selfish and insecure instructors who keep their students jealously bound to them fearing that they will discover other pieces to the puzzle that they don't have. Jeff was an excellent role model for a mentor. A mentor is a trusted teacher or guide as quoted in Webster's dictionary. Besides the deceptively simple definition was an implied relationship of student and master. What the definition failed to describe is the ironic twist that occurs if the relationship was to grow. Sometimes the change could be powerful, and mature, the wise and trusted guide would change into the student and the student into the guide.

The student who is now becoming knowledgeable is interested enough to ask questions and even think of unique ways to approach a problem. If the mentor rejects the student's ideas often, the relationship will be changed. Even though our lives added more demands with finishing degrees, working, and learning new aviation skills, we were to visit Jeff several times. We visited him at a famous hotel for high teas and spent many fascinating afternoons. Jeff always happily beamed, holding his unlighted pipe and listening attentively to all the details.

Through Jeff's encouragement I made an important discovery a few miles down the road in Jerez that accepted students and still does. There can be no greater thrill than to ride the fine movements of the classical high school of dressage. There is no way a trainer can train adequately without ever experiencing the finished product. It is within all the simple movements that one finds the essence of the art of high school that masters such as Xenophon wrote. The more one discovers about the basic halt the more one knows about the advanced skill of piaffe. It is the horse that teaches as the master of the Vienna School, Podhajsky stated, and this is true.

When the magnificent Jerezano did passage and changes into the piaffe it was performed by subtle, fine understanding of the aids through the rider that allowed this astonishing communication. He was truly an excellent teacher by finding the horses and creating the lesson I had to experience to become the skill trainer/rider. He would always say the position is everything, so I brought several of my horses that were in training to work with him. I would ride the horse first and then he would ride the horse and fix my mistakes. Again, I would ride the horse and try to feel and remember the changes in position he made. As I sat and watched him effortlessly work the horses, I would be next to ride and would watch the rider aids carefully. It always looked so easy that I had the impression this ride would be a piece of cake. It never failed that I worked myself into a sweat doing the same thing that he did effortlessly. The secret of the master: simplify. He demonstrated this art when he flew a small plane back with Ernie and me to a small field in Portugal. Upon taking the controls, he was easily able to fly the plane totally steady without the overcorrection often made by beginning pilots. Experts in any field share some of the same skills. Learning to fly was another skill where it soon became evident that doing too much was an excuse of not understanding the skill. A mark of any expert is performing effortlessly most endeavors.

Skilled tasks require mastery of small details. In aviation, some of the skills require the pilot to keep the plane at a specific altitude. One of the exercises is called turns around a point; the pilot turns the airplane while keeping the tip of the wing in place. The other part is that the plane shouldn't deviate up or down. It is similar to the pirouette on horseback whereby the horse pivots with the hind legs in place. The additional problem is that the horse must keep a regular beat of the canter (commonly called gallop) and not only letting the horse swing the hindquarters around but rather staying on a spot. Both these skills take much concentration.

While observing an expert perform either of these skills it appears easy. Perhaps the reason is that beginning to learn any skill demands focus on the ability itself. After many years, provided these skills were well-learned, the expert uses every sense for their performance, because they don't even have to think about the skill. In fact, they often have difficulties teaching because they can't explain how they do it. After learning the rudimentary skills, the expert is able to use all their senses to turn it into an art.

During a visit to Francisco's farm we visited Nuno Oliveira at Quinto do Brejo. As we drove up the long driveway to the indoor arena perched on the side of a hill, we heard beautiful operatic music. It was interesting to see him working with several students in much the same fashion that I experienced. The Portuguese masters as it turns out followed the same principles I was to discover, as I have repeated several times in this book. A friend gave me one of the books that Oliveira had self-published that included a picture of him riding a horse, named Chico, which he helped import to the United States. There have been other books published that are available through publishers. In keeping with many of the classical masters, Oliveira (1982) stated, "Most important, my demands should not exceed the horse's ability to understand and he should be left at the end with the wish to continue to do more than I ask of him" (p.7).

CHAPTER 24

The Sand Pit

Another temporary home- Petrushka helps with chores.

During all my years living in Europe and being dependent on various places to board my horses, we were exposed to the fantastic and to the grotesque. One of the boarding places that we had named the "sand pit" was the now uncared for summer home of a Spanish sherry company owner. The stalls themselves were large and had been well-built using cement and with Dutch doors, which allowed the horses to look out. The stalls were located on the back of a property that had a large, rundown, previously extravagant house that overlooked the Mediterranean. A rather unsavory relative of the family lived down the road in this house. Near the entrance of this property lived a caretaker who collected the rent for the six stables and did work for the debauched relative. Even though many famous sherry families had centuries of unbelievable wealth and fame, this "began to change in the early 1980s when a combination of bad planning and poor timing left many family businesses easy prey for multinationals on the prowl for bargains" (Lorant, 1988). The names were familiar, but in most cases they were owned outside the famous families.

The six stalls were rented to whoever would pay a fairly high rent. The dutiful, but as it turns out forgetful, caretaker was in charge of collecting the stall rent, which we paid in cash. Suddenly we received a note from the Puerto Santa Maria office that we hadn't paid the stall rent. The Osborne bodega that smelled of sherry was located on a narrow street in the small town of Puerto Santa Maria. I walked into the antiquated building and asked to see Sr. Osborne. I was ushered into a historic office on the second floor where he sat behind a sizeable desk. Quickly explaining that cash was given to the caretaker of the property, I produced the scraps of handwritten paper receipts for all the previous months when the money was left at his small house at the designated area near his door. I had never received the normal scraps of paper receipts for the last two months.

It was typical for the old caretaker to spend much of his time at the local café nearby, so there is a good chance he miscalculated the rent. This picturesque bar and restaurant had a stream of customers from early morning until late. They arrived in the morning for café and *copas* of brandy, continuing on to the big midday lunch, and then to the evening of tapas and sherry. These Spanish places were nothing similar to American bars. They were the center of the local social life. Folks didn't go there so much to drink but to talk about the latest news. Even the American school teachers from the nearby Rota Naval Station had their happy hour here. The *Faisan Dorado*—the golden pheasant—was a popular place.

The solution for the old forgetful caretaker was decided that since I had a Spanish bank, where I did all the money transactions to provide security deposits for the horse trips made out of Spain, the money would be sent directly. Meeting him in this formal historic atmosphere was as if I had stepped back several centuries to when many of the sherry businesses started in 1730.

Since I had little interest in sherry, I had no idea at the time that I had just met the man who kept their legendary winery together. According to Lorant (1988), Osborne board member Enrique Osborne said his family was able to retain ownership of the business it has run in nearby Puerto Santa Maria since 1778 because managers were quick to recognize the potential of brandy.

Shenandoah, our Andalusian mare, occupied one stall. At one point the three stalls on the opposite side were rented by a group of racetrack owners that relocated their horses from Madrid for the summer months. Their summer is spent in the cooler weather of the beach towns of the southern Spanish Mediterranean coast and away from the heat of Madrid. The added incentive was the lucrative sport of racing their horses on the nearby beach. Every day the two older racehorses and the young filly were ridden down a nearby road that allowed entry to the beach.

The beach was a popular place to ride horses. We often rode the horses on the beach with Tikki, our lovely and happy Great Dane. She was a wonderful companion with the horses and loved to run alongside them. We picked times when there weren't sunbathers and there were stretches of the beach where it was isolated, such as the place where the beautiful unicorns were photographed by the famous photographer Robert Vavra.

On one of the days when the racehorses took off on their exercise trek, an unfortunate accident happened. They were walking to the entrance of the beach when a dog suddenly jumped out at the horses, scaring the young filly. She fell on the hard paved road and had a deep gash. They brought her back and tossed her into her stall where they brusquely left her.

Because we had a friend who knew the racehorse owners, we found out about the upsetting situation of the young mare. He was very distressed but could do nothing. So, it came to pass that we knew of their interest to rid themselves of the mare. Our navy friend, who formerly had ridden racehorses in California, helped broker the deal to purchase the lovely thoroughbred. She was immediately transferred to the now newly additionally rented stall next to Shenandoah. The wound was immediately cleaned and the vet was called. It was short of a miracle, since it had been left dirty and bleeding for five days, that we were able to get the injury to heal. Luckily there was no damage to her leg, but the pretty mare was left with an ugly-looking wound that would have easily healed if it had been promptly stitched. It had a happy ending and this unsightly wound finally healed with constant care. As you will later read, Petrushka as she was named, traveled with us to Portugal, Northern Spain, and to Germany.

Since the quality of the arena was poor, the sand pit could only be used for limited exercise of my two horses and it wasn't suitable for serious work. The sand pit was fairly deep and for very short exercise wouldn't be harmful. In one positive respect for short exercise, the sand would be helpful because it was soft.

Shenandoah would occasionally do some light work in the sand pit to stay in condition when it wasn't possible to walk to the better grass field. The edge of the farm bordered a street with several houses that faced the arena where we would work, so one of the houses was in plain sight of the arena. Shenandoah and I were happily cantering around the arena when suddenly as we came around, I saw several characters kick in the front door of the facing house. Immediately we walked down the short driveway to the road in front of the house to see what was happening. We were just turning onto the road in front of the house when the characters came running out the front door with their arms loaded with things they had just robbed. They started to run to the back of the house that had a large open field behind it. It was obvious they were going to cross this field to get to their parked car, which was on the other side of the large field. Shenandoah was very easy to canter and as they ran to the back of the house, we followed the fleeing crooks. We had now gained distance and they became aware that something was quickly following them. Shenandoah's pounding hoofs must have sounded as if the mounted troops were after them because they suddenly threw everything down and ran to their car and drove off. The police were called and all the stolen items were retrieved. The thieves were apprehended because in their hast to escape the "wild horse," one of them lost their wallet and were easily identified. The military family who rented the house brought Shenandoah a bag of carrots.

For long sessions, however, it would be too tiring and risk of overextension of the horses to work for extended periods in the deep footing. My coach and I were able to find a level grass field nearby that would allow longer periods of safe exercise on a surface that wasn't too hard or too soft…but was almost just right. It was providence to find an excellent coach who was the director of the large Spanish equestrian center in Jerez. Eventually as I continued my quest to become a good rider, I was privileged to ride in many excellent riding arenas and eventually created two arenas of my own when we returned to the US. It was also the excellent beginning of two exceptional trainers that I easily found coaches when we moved to Germany.

The timeline of life often has a wonderful way of providing opportunities. And so it was that from the wonderful chance to study with Jeff at his riding classes in Seville, through him that I was then introduced to a classical riding master running the Domecq School in Jerez, where I continued riding. The comparison was the sand pit where I now had two outstanding horses to learn how to classically train and an opportunity of a lifetime. If any piece of the timeline had been missing; such as getting permission to enter the exclusive club at the Seville racetrack to attend Jeff's riding classes; or the Portuguese communist revolution that made it impossible for my coach to train horses in Portugal but have to leave for Spain; then none of the rest of the story would have happened. I would have missed the opportunity to work with two exceptional equestrians.

The riders I was lucky to train with considered the riding arena extremely important for the quality of work and also the health of the horse. During this wonderful period, I never experienced horses with problems because of the surfaces they worked on. I was to experience this problem later with a horse that I purchased, not realizing that his owner wasn't careful about the horse's work footing.

Life at the sand pit continued peacefully with few interruptions. Renting the stalls was temporary until I could find a better situation. Always trying to find a place to board horses became a constant struggle. The horses either had wonderful stabling and we had access with trainers who worked at the top levels of dressage expertise or the other extreme. Some of the boarding, such as the sand pit, certainly provided challenging situations. Looking back made me very aware of the wonderful places we enjoyed as we joked that this was better than the sand pit.

One potentially dangerous occurrence happened at the sand pit and seriously threatened one of the horses. The stalls were made of cement as many Spanish buildings were, so they stayed cool during hot weather. We provided all the care for my horses, which meant I fed them before I went to teach and cleaned their stalls after I finished the daily exercise. My students often questioned me about the hay on my clothing. One evening before sunset, I was tidying Petrushka's stall when I became aware of a small animal that seemed to be the size of a cat. It seemed to be moving along the wall on the side away from the door. It probably crept in while we were out riding around the sand pit. I grabbed a rake and tried to shoo the animal out the door. My horse was busy eating so she didn't want to leave. I continued to try and chase this hiding animal out of the stall. At this point, I anxiously realized this wasn't a harmless cat. The small brown creature continued to frantically run along the back wall refusing to be chased out the opened door. My mare was still calm with all this chasing and continued her meal. Unsuccessfully the chase was continued when it occurred to me that this animal wasn't healthy or safe to be in the stall with my mare. As I chased more aggressively, the brown creature began to leap out of the hay with bared teeth and hissing.

During this time, Spain had rampant wild animal sickness including tetanus and rabies, especially in southern Spain. Horses normally aren't at risk as were dogs, but it was clear by the radical behavior that this creature wasn't okay. It was getting closer to sunset and I didn't have any other safe place to stable my horse since Shenandoah was in the next stall. This wasn't safe to leave this most likely sick animal in the stall with my horse. With no phones, and the caretaker who normally had a pellet gun to chase unwanted varmints from the farm wasn't around. I continued to try to rid the stall of this increasingly disagreeable invader. Normally rats aren't aggressive and according to information they would try to leave any provoking situation, especially out an open door. When I realized I couldn't leave it there with my mare, lest she might be bitten if she lay down later as she was accustomed to do in her nicely bedded and safe stall, something had to be done. Horses when they have a safe, quiet stall with deep bedding will sleep lying on their side totally relaxed. The mare was given more of her favorite hay and put in the fenced sand pit where she happily continued munching. Shenandoah called to her from the neighboring stall because she couldn't figure out why she wasn't joining in this extra feast.

The difficult decision was made; it was grim but in view of the safety of my mare, it was made using the large heavy shovel that was found standing near the stall. The intruder was removed and Petrushka was safely and peacefully again in her stall. All was serene at the sand pit.

CHAPTER 25

The Soggy Rat Trap and a Fairy Godmother

Maria Victoria's beloved horse

Almost a year of anxious waiting; it's all over and Petrushka is next to Xierxo in her stall just as if nothing happened. She is happily spending most of the time licking and rubbing her nose on the door, a habit that she had learned in Spain. What happened between the two moments of being at peace with the two horses doing our normal routines of feeding, cleaning, and training? There was the stress of trying to make things normal again. Each time a new boarding place had to be found it was difficult and this problem would have to repeat several more times before we reached our final home.

This happy ending all came about because of another wonderful horse lover who handled many difficult problems on Petrushka's and Xierxo's behalf in my absence. I had suddenly received a transfer to Germany at the end of the school year. Even though the many arrangements had been made, suddenly African Horse Sickness closed our escape from Spain. Again, there was another fairy godmother who softened an impossible situation. Traveling over European borders necessitated many papers and complicated procedures: the horse sickness that almost shut down the Barcelona Olympics made it now impossible.

We were to meet a wonderful new horse friend when we ended up at another new stable. Shortly after Petrushka and I arrived at this stable she became ill with what the veterinarian thought was colic. He treated her with various drugs to relieve any discomfort. Horses don't do well with a series of changes in food. Since I didn't have any control of what she ate at this new stable, there was a strong possibility that her diet wasn't ideal. To ensure that she wouldn't need to be walked or additional care, I decided to sleep in her stall. There was a payphone outside and I had enough change so I could call Ernie for a few minutes as he tried to encourage me. Ernie would later tell me when I had called to tell him I was alone at the new stable that he was so worried because he knew there was no way he could get there from Germany. I had to keep enough change to be able to call the vet in the event she took a turn for the worse.

Here I was curled up in the corner of her stall in the middle of the night. It was the strange feeling of being totally alone except for the comforting and peaceful sounds of all the horses, with their soothing sounds of calm breathing. Soon I settled into the sleeping bag I had thankfully brought along. The hours passed and Petrushka thankfully seemed to be recovered and eating, which was a good sign. Suddenly around two a.m., there was a rustling in the nearby hay. At first it was so quiet I had to strain to make sure I was hearing this rustling sound. Waiting to try and hear where this sound suddenly came from, I was aware not only of the sound but the movement of the hay. The movement now revealed many pairs of staring, inquisitive eyes. Striving to figure out what was causing this disturbance it soon became obvious that the barn was now being overrun with hundreds of rats. I froze in my corner, now they were obvious as they hunted any of the grain Petrushka and the other horses forgot. It was scary not to know what would happen next but as I watched, it all seemed to be nothing more than a busy shopping day at the local market. Petrushka kept eating her hay without any concern, while the orderly shoppers checked out the groceries. Now I quietly leaned back and observed the methodical shoppers doing their daily task. This scene played for several hours when suddenly it all stopped and there were only the sounds of the horses. My shock quickly changed to relief as Petrushka seemed her normal self and this now appeared as a mild discomfort from the change in food. I was able to call Ernie again to relieve his worry about us.

My new friend and I were both teachers and loved animals. She and her mother were involved in rescuing animals. After we survived being under six inches of water, we both began to work on a plan to find a better stable.

It all started when we boarded in a new place in Zaragoza, Spain. After many hours spent stable hunting with fellow horse-lover Maria Victoria, we found a little place actually close to where I taught. Conveniently it was also a short distance from where she taught science and math at a private school close by in the city of Zaragoza. We had spent hours driving around the countryside searching every available place to board horses. We literally went door to door talking to any horse owners and checking anyplace that anyone said there was possible horse boarding, or her Spanish friends that heard there was someplace.

We were desperate to leave the place where we had originally met. It seems more than providence that things happened in a certain way because if they didn't happen there would have been an empty life space. Meeting Maria Victoria in a horrible place that occasionally was underwater when it rained, through this coincidental meeting because of our concern for our horses made a big influence in both our lives. This changed the level in the care of both our beloved horses.

Here we were finally at the cozy but small stable of Garapinillos. All the stalls faced a lovely riding area and the traditional Dutch doors so the horses could look out. When Zaragoza was hit by the high winds, *"lavante"* as they were called, that regularly whirled down the valley, everyone stayed inside. The horses' doors were closed to protect them from the high amount of dust. These notorious *lavantes* stayed for days and by the time they finished it was like the silence experienced when you walk out of a disco. All you could think about was the peace and quiet and not having dust and dirt in every corner of the house and having your car door torn off if you faced the wrong way while getting out.

This was, however, one of the nicest places that we boarded during the two short years I taught school at Zaragoza before I was transferred to Germany. I was always content if my horses had a nice place, but I was a bundle of nerves endlessly looking for another place to board if not. Shortcomings could have been endured in lodging if the horses were safe and happy. The pleasant part of stable hunting was now I had a wonderful friend to share it with, so it was actually fun. Touring the Spanish countryside for a new place was an opportunity because it meant we escaped from the club that we named the "Wet Rat Trap."

CHAPTER 26

Petrushka and Shenandoah
Get a New Home

Kaklak wins dressage competition Estepona, Spain

An acquaintance introduced me to an *aficionado* of horses that lived in Arco, not far from the beautiful town of Jerez de la Frontera. Monolo had a farm filled with Spanish horses of all types. It was situated on the typical unpaved road that seems to lead to most horse establishments. It occurred to me much later that these out of the way dirt roads were a prerequisite for a riding place; it seems there was always a difficult road to navigate to reach the beautiful horses at the end. The exception was the beautiful riding establishment in Germany. Even an exceptional riding club outside of Barcelona, where many of the Olympic horses were boarded, had a two-mile single lane dirt road to get to the club.

At the beginning I rode his already classically trained stallions and in return found a safe haven for my beloved mares Petrushka and Shenandoah. Shenandoah was to have some rest time outside with the pastured mares to recover from an injured hock. The floors of the previous stable were hard cement and even though they were covered with sufficient bedding, Shenandoah had managed to hit the base of her hock, most likely getting up or laying down. Petrushka was going to continue training and was stalled in the main barn, the only mare. And this is how a wonderful period started with working with horses in peace and tranquility. No petty disagreements with club members. I drove every day to the quaint town of Arcos as soon as school finished. Pepe, who cared for the entire farm's horses, was always there to help me get the horses ready to ride.

Later we met another business partner who had several horses at Monolo's farm. This entrepreneur had purchased the trained Lusitano horses from the well-known Portuguese trainer. I was going to help keep them in training and prepare them to be shown at the national competitions. These were the same stallions I had ridden in Portugal. In addition, there were several other stallions, including a large Trakehner and a perfectly proportioned Arabian. There were also the young horses that were bred on this farm. Having escaped the wild happenings at the club, this was a miracle. Monolo had made his home my home in the traditional *"mi casa es tu casa."* And I spent almost every day happily riding all these fantastic horses. My two mares now also had some peace.

Settling into a routine of teaching children and training horses, which shares some similar skills such as teaching single concepts and positively reinforcing that skill, I got in my car to drive the hour roundtrip to Arcos. Riding several horses until nine in the evening I would return home and repeat the whole thing again. Ernie would occasionally accompany me but mostly had a full schedule teaching flying, including the required night flights.

Monolo had a keen eye on the ground even though he no longer had much time for riding. He would come and sit on the patio overlooking the outdoor arena, watching the training and giving comments about the progress. His coaching wasn't limited to the riding session but also additionally helping to perfect my Spanish. I can still hear him say, "No, no Patti," and give the correction. Ernie and I spent many wonderful and pleasurable hours in his home with his delightful family. His wife Maria was a kind woman who always invited me to have something to eat after I finished riding. She made wonderful tortillas, which in Spain are a type of omelet with potatoes. Maria and Mpnolo are some of the most kind and caring people we have known. They opened their home and hearts to two Americans living in their country.

Monolo also opened his home up to other foreigners. There is often an unpleasant aspect to the character of people that newly acquire money; they never trust anyone's motives. They continuingly think that someone is out to get something from them. Many times this may be true, but in the case of Monolo, he didn't have much in the way others would consider riches, but he was rich in other ways. Besides his wonderful family of five boys and two girls, he had a large farm. The foreigner was going to bring cash into the partnership to expand the existing stock of Monolo. We were later to discover the secret behind his wealth and why he stayed in Spain.

The work with the stallions went well and they were to compete in the national shows in Spain. Unfortunately, the foreigner had used his cash for the stallions' purchase, so they were in his control. Both stallions were of the kindest nature and sensitive. The Portuguese rider who trained them was never anything but kind and firm; he didn't have to use force because in the most ways he was an expert. As I was to learn and see repeatedly demonstrated, the true experts don't have to use force because of their excellent skills. The two stallions were responsible for the breeding program at the farm, so in the mornings they performed their breeding duties and stood quietly in the awards presentation, along with the competing mares in the afternoon.

Besides their grand Iberian character, they could be easily ridden by unskilled riders who could hide their ineptness, because these horses are so athletic and talented they can make an unskilled rider look good. Kaklak, the beautifully proportioned Arabian, was overlooked in lieu of the larger stallions. He was lucky because of his size, so no one thought him the flashy horse to show off with. The truth is, he was very talented and won a national dressage competition in Estepona, Spain.

Our iniquitous foreigner, who also turned out to be a frustrated bullfighter, would come to the farm for short visits and take the two large stallions to the local town fiestas where he showed off, making them jump madly around. The tragedy was that both these stallions were so finely trained to perform what in Spanish is called *Alta Escuela,* doing brilliant passage and piaffe, the rider only had to barely think of the exercise, using cues that no one could see. These are the exercises performed by the renowned Lipizzaners of Vienna. After these days of wild rides, the one stallion would appear uninterested in anything in his surroundings and stand in the corner of his stall with his head down and not move. I had come to know this horse extremely well. Horses aren't supposed to reveal emotions; we just don't recognize them. Having raised several stallions, I have learned that they are even more sensitive than mares in many ways. They become very connected to people and recognize a devoted handler. By this time I learned that if I wanted to exist in this culture it was useless to say anything, and the best counsel was to try and make change by quiet example. Looking back, I realize that my coach also abhorred what was being done but being a part of this group, anything he said would have figuratively removed himself from this small horse group. As wrong and outraged as we were about this man, he was the owner. I was to see this scene play out in many countries, both the horrific and the sublime.

All the untalented riders of the world have this in common. One of the truths about the riding masters of the world is that they don't have to use force to train their horses. This is also explained in my area of psychology and education; the use of force is easily resistant. As I have discussed in three other books, people are reinforced by using force. It is only by example that some folks become interested in trying other measures. If you can teach a crocodile to come and perform on cue—need I say more? This is an amazing training session that supports operant training for horses (Wildlife Conservation Society. 2008).

Everything would again be peaceful and quiet and the training would continue as always; the horses were all calm and happy. Wembley was calm and responsive when I entered his stall. Months passed by until "The Owner" reappeared on the scene. Under what appeared to be pleasant conversation, there was constantly the suspicious masked hostility that he thought was hidden but was immediately recognized by my fighter pilot husband and me. Ernie had encountered much wickeder people than "The Owner." He was manipulative in acting friendly but these folks always give themselves away. His true colors burst out uncontrollably in the following episode.

Shortly thereafter, I purchased the wonderful bay Lusitano, Xierxo, from the noted farm outside of Lisbon. This was during the hard economic times of Portugal after the communist takeover when dollars were needed in their economy. He was a gorgeous two-year-old Lusitano. When "The Owner" heard our good news and looked at the picture, all he saw was the resemblance to his horse here on Monolo's farm. His reaction revealed his true malevolent character. He became outraged and the nice friendly demeanor changed. He yelled, "How dare they breed my stallion before they shipped him here." If this idiot had taken one second to perform simple math, he would have realized that the formation of my two-year-old was impossible by his stallion, unless by Immaculate Conception. At this time, the technology we now have thirty-five years later with our horses was unavailable.

Again, social tranquility returned and the original serenity returned as business dealings distracted "The Owner" and he lost interest; he didn't come around anymore. Actually, rumor had it that "The Owner" was in hiding and being sought for internationally smuggling extra items in his international shipments.

Petrushka and Shenandoah had their nice place and I had a great place to ride. We also had the happy news that Shenandoah was expecting a foal.

Shenandoah's new foal- Shembley

CHAPTER 27

Petrushka Can't Come With Xierxo

Xierxo and Fanfare in their new stalls

Life has a way of turning plans upside down. We were doing all the preparation to ship Petrushka and Xierxo to the States for our final destination, when the test results came back for their shipping papers. Petrushka had tested positive for piroplamosis. It was a total shock and we needed some time to accept the sadness that this would change the happy plan of going to our own farm in the States. She wasn't sick but the test supported that at some time she had been exposed to the parasite passed to the horse by biting insects such as ticks and mosquitoes. At this dreadful turn of events we looked to what type of treatment could be of benefit. Even at present, the treatment is still an incredibly difficult chemo-type therapy that even at this writing isn't successful. It was a realistic possibility that she would become sick from the treatment. I was told by several vets that she had produced antibodies most likely in defense of being exposed; the test doesn't differentiate this fact. When one researches piroplasmosis in the United States most writers will assure the reader that it's not endemic. Then why were the European horses coming to the Atlanta-held Olympics in a stage of worry and the Olympic officials in an unbelievable activity to control mosquitoes, the method of transmission? After all, there wasn't any piroplamosis in the United States. There are some possible economic reasons with the importing of Arabian horses that are posited.

Faced with an insurmountable impasse, the energy was now spent on how we would make the best decision. We had just overcome the African Sickness in Spain to get both Petrushka and Xierxo out of Spain, and now again we were faced with another defenseless problem.

One of my horse contacts was a horse lover I had helped when she had purchased a large warmblood from a seller who hadn't told all the facts. This horse had been on the jumping circuit and being an extremely large horse had become too difficult to control on the course. Maggie had purchased him and boarded him at a small local farm. With no safe restricted place to ride, she decided to take him for a walk down a quiet road in the local town. Everything went okay until he was frightened. He turned suddenly and bolted, demonstrating why he had been sold. He was unbelievably strong and Maggie had no control when he quickly bolted. Actually, it was lucky for Maggie when she unceremoniously dismounted, because he was at a full run tearing through the town dodging anything in the way; there was little chance of her safety with her limited riding experience, so this turned out a blessing.

She called me later that day upset about the close call and her miscalculation. I was now boarding my horses at a beautiful, mostly dressage club in Ochsenfurt. They had a beautiful huge indoor arena, outdoor fenced arena, and there were walks along the river too. I outlined a safe plan if she sincerely wanted to safely work with this horse. He and Maggie arrived at the Ochsenfurt club and we began the same techniques that I had learned from my Portuguese master. Just as I had done with the bronco Diablo in Spain, she began to longe him and then finally ride him safely in the restricted indoor arena.

It was a surprise returned favor when Maggie helped me find Petrushka a safe home in Germany. Again, as Maria Victoria and I had toured every inch of the local community, Maggie and I now toured every local club that she could find and finally she found one in Wũrzburg. This was a pleasant place where the Trakehner breed was continued and young people came to learn all aspects of taking care of horses, not only riding. Each student had a young horse to care for besides the horse that they took their riding lesson on. This now became Petrushka's new home. They were overjoyed because she was not only trained but carried the Thoroughbred papers that allowed her to be bred for the Trakehner line.

This is how my life became involved with Trakehners. Petrushka stayed at the German farm and Fanfare was going to the States with Xierxo, thanks to the kindness of another horse lover who again stepped in to lighten my heartache of having to leave her behind and find her a home. My work was to continue in the United States to help horses have a happier life by teaching basic classical methods that allowed their owners a positive, less stressful method of training…but with some surprising differences that I couldn't have anticipated. After all, wasn't working with horses the same?

Our aviation friends introduced us to an agent who specialized in horse transport. This was the first leg of the long trip from the farm in Wũrzburg, to the Frankfurt airport, to Los Angeles, and finally a difficult commercial truck ride to a temporary farm in Washington State. Previously I detailed that the flight was uneventful but since our trailer hadn't arrived in the States, the horses had to be shipped commercially.

We'll never know exactly what happened on the truck ride, but the young two-year-old Fanfare arrived at the farm with a sore hind leg. She was promptly treated by a vet and it was deemed not serious but as time went by she seemed to recover but as we began light exercise on the line and free work she was uncomfortable on her hind leg. Over and over she was evaluated and seemed recover only to become mildly lame which prevented seriously beginning her work.

Xierxo had been in steady work so the trip although arduous wasn't as stressful because he had the muscles to cope with the constant motion. Fanfare was only just two years old, so she hadn't started training and didn't have the muscle stamina. They had three days quiet time for the necessary quarantine in Los Angeles before the truck trip, but this was still a hard, tiring trip that we wouldn't have planned if it hadn't been for the difficulty about Petrushka's testing.

After two temporary boarding farms, we finally had the stalls built and Xierxo and Fanfare had their own home. Since the property only had a huge old barn, everything had to be quickly done, including the prefab house. The two stalls were built inside the over 100-year-old barn and a two-acre pasture were swiftly completed, so life was happy for the horses. The property had been one of three predominant dairy farms in the area and the first to go out of business because of the increasingly difficult regulations. Each of the other two farms has also retired the dairy part of their farms since we arrived from Europe. This was the beginning of the process of building an indoor and outdoor arena, and slowly converting a prefab house from the inside out. It turned out the prefab house was one of our providential decisions because the building permit requirements changed shortly thereafter and we wouldn't have been able to complete a building from a plan as we had in Germany.

CHAPTER 28

Beijing Horses

Beijing horse on The Sacred Way

After more than over twenty years in elementary education, life presented opportunities for a career change. With a strong interest in aviation, human factors, and completing a dissertation in aviation decision making, I began writing research in this area and teaching graduate level classes. Collaborating with Ernie on several topics, I received notification that my research submission for a conference in Beijing, China, was accepted.

We had been traveling all over Europe and Ernie had flown as a fighter pilot in the East, so this would be my first trip to the East and there was great excitement in our preparation for the over week-long trip. Since the farm was a big responsibility, we began to work on gathering several people who would help take care of everyone, including two Great Danes.

The flight over the northern section of Alaska was an eye-opener because instead of this pristine wilderness that the press told us was being destroyed, it appeared that we were looking at the frozen surface of the moon. The flight that had amazing visibility for almost the total flight until we landed in Beijing allowed us to have an incredible view. This was in the middle of November, so everything below was a stark frozen terrain where there wasn't a sign of any living thing of plants or habitation; there wasn't a single sign that anything or anyone lived below in the frozen wasteland. I quietly commented to Ernie who confirmed that we were out of reach of an emergency landing for a long stretch. Pilots are always thinking of where you'd land. The weather over the Bering Sea heading and over Siberia really jarred my reality of what I thought this geography looked like.

The Triple Seven flight that was normally booked full of commuters on the daily direct flight from Seattle to Beijing, was empty because of a holiday. If there were a hundred people on the flight, that was probably an over-estimation of passengers. This huge jet should have had at least three hundred. The three seat rows now had people stretched out sleeping and the crew had plenty of time to walk around and chat with us while handing out glasses of wine.

There was absolutely nothing to see except uninhabited darkness. It was so unlike flying in the United States or Europe where even sparsely unpopulated areas have noticeable lights. Hours passed but Ernie and I had much to talk about when finally the areas of more population came into view as we approached China and the airport of Beijing. The cabin staff that traveled this route now commented excitedly that this was the first time that they had ever been able to see the ground so clearly at this altitude. They went around the cabin alerting people to look out their window. We now started gazing out the window as they pointed out various things on the ground that even at this height were extremely clear. Suddenly an item they pointed out seemed to be a long winding road that at first looked dark as we flew above continuing for miles, but it didn't have any traffic. We suddenly realized we had the perfect view of the Great Wall of China and a view that was rarely seen from this Seattle-Beijing flight. This aerial view was more impressive than the actual trip to see it from ground level.

We had driven all over Europe but as we took the commercial vehicle to the hotel downtown, we were glad we had decided not to drive. How the driver avoided the swarm of small motorcycles and various means of transportation was incredible. How the jumble of all these things moving and not hitting each other was amazing to behold. The week attending the conference was uneventful but several experiences were extremely unique. The attendees could participate in the normal tours but were allowed to be directed by the Chinese research members and participants of the conference. Instead of the normal official Chinese guides who gave the standard, often inaccurate tours, we were fortunate to have a Chinese graduate student escort us around to all the famous locations, including the tombs and the Great Wall.

After the first day our Chinese graduate student guide came to know us as a fellow research conference participant who was also involved with postsecondary education. Our small group was comprised of university professors and researchers. He was interested in our professional backgrounds as he prepared to teach at a Chinese university. The conversations while driving on the private bus included discussions that went beyond what would have been the typical government guides' canned speech. He was asked many searching questions, which he answered carefully but increasingly honestly. His transparent moment revealed that the communist government was encouraging the industrious endeavors and private property, while concerned about supporting a weighty, dependent, retiring population.

Looking back on the information, I see it in a different context and the clear dichotomy of the Chinese government. The memory is that the normal Chinese that you came in contact with couldn't do enough to help you, and acted as if no task was demeaning to perform with honor. This included the driver we hired to take us to several horse farms that I had researched. They were indeed industrious. It would have been impossible to find any of these farms without his help. Horse farms are sometimes as we always joked about, hidden down often impassible roads; these farms would have been incredibly difficult to find if not impossible. Even our driver had to frequently stop and approach locals for directions to find the farms.

Beijing was in that state of full development with the upcoming Olympic Games scheduled to be held in 2008. Actually, the equestrian events were held in Hong Kong and after we visited what were considered the best horse centers near the city of Beijing, they were sorely lacking in the quality of riding establishments that we had seen for smaller private barns all over Europe. There were several imported of the type that would be seen in exclusive competitive barns. I commented to Ernie about the coarse eating hay filled with small dried sticks. These horses would be so lucky to have some of the lush grass-type hay found on our farm. The area was extremely dry and the outdoor arena extremely dusty. During the several trips to the horse farms, the countryside didn't have any of the typical greenery of the farms I was familiar with.

The weather for the first part of our trip and when we did most of the farm tours was clear and cold. This weather radically changed toward the end of the trip while touring in the city of Beijing. The city had what is described as a winter inversion, which makes any pollutants harder to be carried away. The city has heavy pollution because of the mass population and traffic density. In normal weather this is carried away but with the cool air inversion became difficult. We had the surprise to see the whole population of Beijing wearing masks. It felt unreal and while this was to protect the wearers against pollutants, it foreshadowed an ominous future.

The censoring security by the Chinese government at this famous hotel was somewhat a shock when part of an email that had a research paper attached was deleted with information about the removed attachment. Indeed, it was censorship and I was informed that I wouldn't be able to receive any attachments, no matter the educational content.

Another interesting occurrence happened when we kept meeting the same very fit business-looking chap while riding in the elevator to our room and then in the lobby of the hotel. The hotel was in the obvious preparation for receiving a "high level" guest indicated by the red carpet being rolled out in the lobby. Each time we would meet, he chatted with us in a way to elicit information about why we were there. Ernie quickly figured out that they were checking on everyone's background. It turned out to be fun because during one of the "chance" meetings, he invited us to one of their great local restaurants where it was obvious all the US Department of Defense security folks hung out. He couldn't say too much; obvious especially to Ernie he was working on a security detail as an American. We never asked what. This type of covert conversation was definitely out of my experience level, so I followed Ernie's direction. It remains one of the most interesting dinners…talking about everything but nothing in detail. Kind of fun getting a security clearance to get a dinner invite.

While we were both history buffs, Ernie had an undergraduate emphasis in history, so we were apprised of the centuries of difficulties that these opulent edifices represented; no matter how beautiful (https://www.chinafetching.com/timeline-of-chinese-dynasty). After seeing the characteristic tourist attractions and magnificent buildings …it's where are the horses? Following taking pictures at all the royal palaces, it wasn't standing in the now peaceful Tiananmen Square (Gate of Heavenly Peace)that was the highpoint but having Ernie take my picture next to the famous horse on the Emperor Row (Map of Ming Tombs,n.d.)

CHAPTER 29

Lipizzaner Horses

Famous Vienna stallions visit Jerez for a historical reunion with Domecq horses.
This picture was taken at the *Yeguada Militar de Jerez de la Frontera*

Besides the wonderful Lipizzaner horses used in Jeff's riding classes, I had the wonderful opportunity to see the Vienna stallions when they visited the Jerez school. It was during the time that I was studying classical riding in what is presently called the *Real Escuela Andaluza Del Arte Ecuestre*, under the direction of Francisco. The stallions arrived by train and had planned several performances to commemorate the original breeding program. It was a fantastic opportunity to see first-hand the training of the Lipizzaner horses. Already enamored with classical training this was a chance of a lifetime.

Spanish Riding School is the oldest Riding Training academy, especially for the Lipizzan horse breed. The school is located in Vienna, Austria, and was established in 1572 AD by Habsburg Emperor. Spanish Riding School is one of the "Big Four" riding training academies of the world; others are Royal Andalusian School, Portuguese School of Equestrian Art, and Cadre Noir in France (Kawsar, n.d.).

The breeding program began with Spain and Austria in the 16th century, so from the Spanish Andalusian horse began the beautiful Lipizzan horse breed. From this history the present day's events were commemorated. Many people participated in an event that would be memorable because the Lipizzaners travel infrequently. Not only did I see the performances but the training that preceded them. One of the first performances was in the outdoor arena used for many of the national competitions. Even though both the Spanish Riding School horses and the Domecq horses were stallions, there was much loud calling from each group as they performed together. It seemed that some of the stallions believed that mares had joined their group and they needed to get their attention. This was an incredible experience to be an observer to the behind the scenes happenings. Providence would have it that I would meet my next Lipizzaner soon.

We had purchased a beautiful thirty-five-acre farm that had been one of the three major dairy farms in the area with an over 125-year-old barn. It was a fortunate find but the problem was that there was no house for us or stalls for horses. The house was quickly accomplished with a prefab house that eventually became unrecognizable with embellishments, but the stalls took a little longer so we were once again boarding. The only good news was that it was to be accomplished soon because we quickly made contacts that helped us make the transition from a dairy to a horse farm with indoor and outdoor arenas.

Until we could complete this sizable project we boarded the horses at a nearby farm that had a papered Lipizzaner stallion that they were using to begin a breeding program. As mentioned, the Austrian farm often sells the famous horses, which is how Jeff had acquired his two Lipizzaners. Interestingly, no one had ridden this beautiful horse who apparently was well-trained…so the owners thought. Since their primary interest was his breeding potential their interest in his ability to promote him as a breeding stallion was the focus of their horse business.

Our time boarding here was temporary until we could build stalls for Xierxo and his new Trakehner companion Fanfare. Their indoor arena left much to be desired compared to where I had recently ridden, but it was only temporary. After they watched me ride Xierxo several days, they decided that they had found someone to try their Lipizzaner and approached me with the idea. I never assume anything about horses because of all my serious training, so I began to evaluate him on the classical longe work to see how he moved without a rider and if he could make transitions easily to each gait. They had never seen anyone work this way and assumed I would just jump on cowboy style. After all, if you're a good rider that's what you do.

This was the beginning of the realization that horse training wasn't the same here in the United States. They called it dressage but it was really Western riding in an English saddle. There weren't the standard principles that I experienced in Europe. They approached me with a business deal to board my horses and I would ride their Lipizzaner and show him at the upcoming stallion show.

Stallion Show

The stallion show was to present eligible breeding potential. Each year the local stallion owners presented their horses. Since the arena was fairly close, we went several days to practice and get him comfortable with the place. There weren't many distractions during the day, only several horses quietly being ridden. It was a favorable plan but didn't duplicate the arena filled with noisy spectators with bright lights. The evening for the performance came and we warmed up in a small arena next to the large doors to the arena where we'd entrance. Some of the cheering inside reached us but I knew as soon as that large door opened and we entered he would be faced with bright lights and cheering. The moment now came, the doors were opened, and he willingly walked in and halted on command. It was noisy, but now the audience erupted loudly into a cheer; he suddenly startled and abruptly moved in a circle. It must have looked erratic because the announcer boomed, "Looks as if we'll see some riding now!"

Only two of the stallions were presented under saddle with most running free, being chased by their owner, or on a line running in a circle. There was only one other stallion being ridden. Unknown to us was that this was the young Hungarian stallion that would be the future sire for my German mare. They were seriously working to prepare him for competitions. For several seconds I allowed the white stallion to pause, and when he then relaxed we started the routine. He was a wonderful horse and surely he had begun his training as all the stallions from my coaches, especially my Portuguese trainer who not only had advanced horses but many that began their first lessons.

Many business arrangements proceed and transitions are consistent for a time. They knew I had contact with my German coach as he traveled doing clinics throughout the US. They were happy when I made the arrangements for him to teach several days at their farm. They even did some work on the dusty arena in preparation for the clinic. He was also able to help them start one of their young Lipizzaners. The horse had been taught all the basic work of the rider commands on the longe line. The next step was missing. We needed a quiet rider and someone who had excellent longe skills for the next introduction. My German coach fit the bill. During the four-day clinic we introduced this nice quiet Lipizzaner to the equestrian world. These riders had a preconception that horses being ridden for the first time buck and do horrible things. During the three summers I brought my horses to Portugal and also rode the young horses beginning training. I never had or saw the horses misbehave because they were so consistently and quietly worked they didn't know anything else.

Just as aviation folks can walk onto the flight operations and without talking to anyone knows the quality of the personnel, I could walk into an arena and tell you about the level of the riders. If you're willing to ride on an uneven, rutted, dusty surface it means that your understanding of the skills is limited. Because as dancers need excellent floors, so do the horses. When my German friend arrived, the arena had some new footing…it now was deep in wood chips that hid the hard dirt below.

It was pleasant for us to again meet our German friend who we had spent so many enjoyable days with at his German farm where my horses were boarded. He had made an important move to the United States. This was his new business and he had excellent skills for dealing with his clients. He now had changed his teaching format to traveling around to various farms instead of working strictly from his own farm as he had in Germany. In Germany, his clients mostly had their horse in training and rarely came to ride their horse. However, I rode my horses everyday and instead of him riding my horse, he coached me training my own horses. It was another fantastic opportunity.

The disagreeable part came when he wanted to spend an evening social time with Ernie and me on our farm talking about our shared experience and catch up since we had all returned to the States. We also had arranged several group get-togethers because several of the clinic students wanted to ride their lesson in our new outdoor arena, rather than in the newly renovated dusty arena that now had about a foot of wood chips.

The Lipizzaner Lady made this so unpleasant because they thought with my background I would of course be starting a horse training business and try to steal my German coach. Even though they were told, they couldn't understand or believe that I was seriously working on finishing a dissertation in aviation human factors and had no interest in doing a horse training business. In fact, all the people I had helped with their horses never paid me for my coaching. So *déjà vu* here we are back in Spain stepping on someone's "Horse Business."

I still am good friends with my German coach and have sent several horse friends living back east to work with him. With my own farm at least, my horses are also safe. The real experts in any field aren't threatened but rather interested to talk with others in their field. Ernie and one of his graduate students had the opportunity of interviewing the famous German ace Hartmann. He couldn't have been more gracious with his time and viewed it as a way of sharing the aviation he loved. This behavior is typical of truly outstanding experts in any endeavor.

It's a psychological mystery why folks behave in this manner, but protectiveness doesn't move someone to positive happenings. The horse industry doesn't have a corner on this market, but like aviation it's a small community. It's hard to go anyplace and not meet someone you know.

Being kind of quiet about all my really lucky past activities, it came about that the Lipizzaner Lady was contacted by the famous horse photographer to include photos of their classic Lipizzaner in his upcoming book. As I arrived one morning and was offered coffee, she chirped the news that this famous photographer wanted to photograph their Lipizzaner. Coincidence? I had never mentioned anything more than he was a fantastic photographer who produced beautiful pictures of Spanish horses and how fortunate she was when the telephone suddenly rang. Lipizzaner Lady answers the phone and after talking about the horse photos suddenly says, "Oh, a friend of yours from Spain is here." She thinks the little I've mentioned about knowing him couldn't mean that this famous photographer will remember me. For sure this is some embellishment on my part and my subterfuge will be shown. Remember the chapter about the unicorns? I never mentioned any of that. If you also remember my description of him you'll know what happened next.

You know there are people who create such a positive influence that they are not only memorable for their quiet brilliance but influence your life in positive ways. Robert "Bob" Vavra is not only a wonderful photographer but loves what he does and he conveys a gracious, kind-to-all-around-him persona that we experienced while we worked with photographing the unicorns in Spain. So, he said, "Wonderful…let me speak with Patti."

CHAPTER 30

Fanfare Starts a New Life

Petrushka with her beautiful foal

Quarantine for horses is difficult at best. Xierxo was fortunate because we had him gelded before his international trips to spare him even longer quarantine times. Even though he had to stay in the States for three months before traveling back to Europe, the hardest was the month that he was confined to his stall for the quarantine, but he didn't have to endure daily testing. Fanfare, if she had been over two years old, would have had extremely unpleasant three-month quarantine at The Center for Equine Health at UC Davis. These regulations are always in flux depending not only on the important health issues but horse politics; which powerful horse groups want to exclude another.

Petrushka was fortunate to stay in Germany taking into account that she would have been considered a potential breeding mare and had to endure constant testing for the three-month quarantine. Xierxo was happy to at least be left alone for the month quarantine and then back to normal at the lovely trotter farm. This time Fanfare was less than two-years-old and Xierxo was a gelding, so after their three days in quarantine at the Los Angeles station they were allowed to be trucked to Washington. Unfortunately, this drive was made in one non-stop trip, during one of the harshest storms.

Several years later, I returned to Germany to purchase two Trakehner geldings. Petrushka was still happily there and had produced a beautiful foal. The farm owner and his wife accompanied the two new horses and they didn't fare as well on the flight because their caretakers couldn't be bothered to go back to the cargo section directly behind their seats to give them water. Both horses were extremely dehydrated when we saw them off-loaded at the Los Angeles quarantine station for their three-day stay. This time the remaining part of their trip was in my control with their comfortable German trailer and an overnight stop halfway to Washington, so they wouldn't have to endure the same trip as Fanfare and Xierxo.

Now the farm had been busy building new stalls, a prepared outdoor arena, and an indoor arena. Everything was readied for the beginning of a new horse adventure...this time it was all ours.

CHAPTER 31

Firefox Russian Orlov-Rostopchin

Firefox Orlov-Roshopchin

During year 1999 as history set a new trajectory for Russia, again economics entered the influential changes on the horse industry. Several horse lovers became involved with some Americans who were interested in the Russian breed of the Orlov- Rostopchin and became involved in importing them. Because of the typical economic impact on Russia, Russian breeders were anxious to sell for foreign currencies such as the dollar. The economic situation once again repeated.

In the course of 1998, the outbreak of a severe banking, currency and sovereign debt crisis could not be prevented. The Russian stock, bond and currency markets collapse as a result of fears for a ruble devaluation and a default on domestic debt.

(The Russian Crisis 2013).

Once again, the horse industry was distressed and Russian breeders with breed lines of several hundred years began to sell their top stallions for dollars and just the way I had acquired the beautiful Lusitano, Xierxo. A beautiful Russian Orlov-Rostopchin stallion was shipped to the United States through Amsterdam, and eventually ended up on our farm in Washington State, with his owner. When the beautiful German Trakehner failed to stay ready for continued dressage training, the idea to breed this beautiful stallion with the lovely German mare was decided. The German Trakehner mare and Russian stallion breeding was exactly the program to continue these famous lines.

There were never thoughts about becoming involved with breeding; it was outside of what I considered my expertise. The experience of witnessing the expert handling of the two stallions Palpite and Wembley performing their duty often before they were dispatched to compete in the afternoon competitions portended the seriousness of this skill. Pepe knew every horse and was amazing in his quiet handling of the horses. Frankly, I never considered how amazing the training by the Portuguese master of these two stallions was. They had been so well trained that they separated the two different environments. I normally practiced with the two stallions in an outdoor arena at Monolo's farm in close proximity to the herd of mares grazing nearby. Occasionally there was a call of greeting and they immediately began their work.

Looking back on the breeding on the Spanish farm with the handler, I realize the difficulty and the expertise involved with Pepe the stallion handler. After knowing about several stallion breeding accidents, this fact was glaringly clear. One of the factors at the Spanish farm was it was a closed group; no strange horses being brought in to breed; the horses all knew each other. Consequently, it appears, that the spontaneous breeding of my mare and the Russian sire went so easily was aside from the mare being ready to breed was because the horses were accustomed to each other being stalled somewhat near.

Almost a year later we had the first foal born on the farm, Fanfare and Xierxo were always pastured together outside when the weather was pleasant. Otherwise, they all had extra-large stalls, especially Fanfare, in the event that she should foal while inside. It was a beautiful day, so the two horses were turned out in their large grass field in the morning. Several hours later upon checking on them there was a third horse running around. It was truly amazing…this little guy just standing there. Firefox, as he was named for the fast supersonic Russian fighter plane, was the first of three horses born on the farm.

During the time that Firefox's dad was on the farm he was easy to handle and ride. He returned to his home and sadly was euthanized after a breeding accident. Firefox continued his training and became especially talented doing several tricks and being uncharacteristically smart and different from most typical horse talents. He became amazingly talented at opening stall doors. He also snake-like slithered out of the open part of his Dutch door. If I hadn't seen him, I wouldn't have believed it. He put his front legs through the open top part and then leaned through the door until his front feet touched the ground, letting his hind legs follow. Now standing in front of his stall he looked at me as to say, "What do you think of my new trick?" Fearing he had hurt his back legs, I walked over to him to make sure he was okay. He immediately stood at attention, performing to get a carrot. He truly had untypical horse smartness that mostly we accredit to dogs.

Again, economics had entered and ruined the horse industry, but this time in favor for those importing Russian horses. Since horse sports and hobby activities are dependent on discretionary income, people need to have extra money for fun activities. We live near a military base that has miles of land used for training. The troops were finding many horses running around the potential training areas. Folks who would trailer into nearby areas to trail ride came back to their horse trailer to find a horse tied to the side. The horse industry was again in economic crises and people couldn't afford the extra cost. This hit every aspect of the economy. We were also avid sailors with a sailboat at a local marina. Normally to get a boat slip was difficult and someone had to bequeath you their slot. Now the marina was only a third full. The smaller power boats that families used for fun days and fishing were nonexistent. One popular holiday when the harbor would be filled with boats had the harbor virtually empty of any celebrating boats.

At this point there wasn't any future in breeding either the Trakehner or the Orlov-Rostopchin stallions. These two stallions had several hundred years of history. Firefox's dad had been scored a perfect ten in the Russian confirmation tests. This stallion wouldn't have been sold if not for the Russian economics, so this has to have been tragic to sell him for what only amounted to a few thousand dollars. Even though both of these stallions were easy to handle, they still needed attention. At this point I made the difficult decision to geld both even though there wasn't any reason due to their behavior. It was just to make the logistics of allowing them less restrictions; they could now be free to be pastured with mares. It was a tremendously difficult decision but there wasn't any reasonable breeding possible.

Breeding was never the main consideration of the farm. Now the knowledgebase of the significant loss of breeding lines of several hundred years seemed ominous. The decision was delayed for a long time. The breeding program was merely a coincidence of Fanfare's unsoundness for dressage with the arrival of the Russian stallion on the farm. Otherwise, there wouldn't have been the attention paid to the German mare Fanfare's sire Harnish nor the Russian sire of Firefox.

Recently if the reader searches for the specifics of the Orlov-Rostopchin breed it will be noted that it has become an assortment of Russian breeds. With recent economic pressures as of this writing, many of the Russian websites used for my references are not presently available.

CHAPTER 32

Flying Horses and Great Danes

Tikki Jump

While living in Germany during my first teaching assignment, I met another American who was an exchange student teaching at a local German high school. Her fiancé who eventually became her husband was finishing a doctorate with the University of Heidelberg. A fellow colleague had presented him with a purebred Great Dane, Irma. He kept her in the hallway of the university's staff housing. As typical of how many Great Danes are placed in new homes because their owners are no longer able to care for them, soon by chance I owned and loved my first Great Dane. Irma loved the huge German farm and had a wonderful although short life. Because Great Danes are so big, often weighing as much as a full-grown man, they often are not long lived.

The next teaching assignment was Spain and many new animals came into my life. Besides the horses, a Great Dane named Tikki came into our lives and she loved running on the beach with the horses. She is the Great Dane who is pictured jumping up to touch my hand. None of our horses were ever afraid of the Danes. After her passing we didn't have any Great Danes until we returned to the States and we could have our own large, protected farm. We owned a lovely home in Germany with a fairly large yard but because of our hectic schedule of teaching, flying, and riding horses, it was time demanding. To have a dog that needed attention wasn't fair, so this was the period of cats.

My mother was always rescuing cats and dogs and decided that she had the perfect cat for us. On her next visit we owned the cat named Princess. She was totally happy and ended up with a companion. The new cat was a doll-faced German Persian that belonged to my dear friend Inger, who besides feeding all the homeless cats in her neighborhood had a male doll-faced Persian cat. When she was rewarded with pick of the litter she presented this beautiful kitten to me with the words, "I know since you take all of your animals wherever you go, you wouldn't sell this precious cat." The last time she had pick of the litter she presented the kitten to a friend who promptly turned around and sold her.

Yes, Inger was right and this kitten traveled back to the States along with Princess sitting in their carrier in a place directly behind the horse stall boxes on the combination flight. These combination flights had the front part with the normal passengers and toward the back of the plane there was the service galley with a cargo section right behind this service section. The accompanying woman and her daughter who had one box of horses and a German Sheppard and I sat in the last row next to the galley. What none of the passengers realized was that right behind this food service were six horses, one dog, and two cats, and a huge box of birds that had nothing to do with us.

I had been booked on a commercial cargo flight but my German agent, Guido Klatte, said that this would be much more comfortable. This company still internationally transports horses and simplifies everything. All I had to do was to look after the third horse in the box with my two horses, Xierxo and Fanfare. At the Lufthansa cargo terminal where the horses were prepared to load we were given a briefing and practice about how to handle the huge cargo net between the cargo locked on the plane's frame and the passenger section. This is an aviation security in the event of a sudden stop. We have a safety net in the SUV so that when the vehicle might have a sudden stop, Allie the resident Great Dane is safe sitting stretched out on the seats behind the driver. She would be protected from being tossed over the front seat by this similar aviation-style cargo net. We had to demonstrate the opening and safe closing of this cargo net in a preflight safety briefing while on the ground, so during the actual flight we could get access to the horses.

After the plane reached altitude, we were allowed to go to the cargo section, which we entered through a door hidden in the back of the galley. Casually looking at the service counters wouldn't have indicated that here was anything unusual about this place except that it had a hidden section in the tail. The other horse owner and I anxiously went back to the horses to make sure that they were all calm. The take-off had been very smooth so I wasn't too concerned. When we navigated through the opening of the cargo net and arrived at the horse boxes, they were all munching hay. Because this was in January the flight was with the aloft winds and it was a direct flight from Frankfurt to Los Angeles.

The remaining part of the flight was uneventful; we never had any need for all the tranquilizers that both of us carried. During the trip we went to the horses especially to make sure they had water and didn't get dehydrated. This was actually more important than the hay that we frequently gave. Returning to our seats after one of these trips someone sitting in the seats ahead had noticed our group comings and goings. This time with some noticeable hay on our clothing we were asked what was going on behind the galley. When we replied that we were just feeding the horses—I'm not sure he believed us.

Life on our new farm with Xierxo and Fanfare in their new homes was the beginning. And several more horses followed from Germany and several horses were born on the farm. Then came the Danes!

In my heart I missed Irma and Tikki but didn't remember this feeling. When I went to visit a horse farm at the request of one of my students and saw a huge Great Dane, my memories all flooded out; this was the beginning. Immediately I had to find out where this Great Dane came from and found out he was deaf and had been rescued. Before we knew it, we were rescuing a sweet, soulful-looking merle Great Dane called Misty; this is how the new wonderful line of Great Danes came to pass.

The next Great Dane came to the farm when a university colleague was moving to Alaska. She was living in Hawaii and her older son who leash-walked Sebastian was also leaving. When the travel crate was opened and he jumped out, he stood for several seconds appraising the fact that he wasn't on a leash and was free. The front of the thirty-five-acre farm has five-foot fencing so Sebastian would be safe. In seconds he was running around the house and the nearby barn at full speed. After he made several circles he finally came and sat in front of us as if to say, "That was fun!" From then on he was free to run and only had to be on a leash to visit the vet. He and Misty were fast friends spending several happy years until Misty passed away in her sleep. Days passed and Sebastian was inconsolable and basically stopped eating. It was time to rescue another Great Dane.

CHAPTER 33

Star: The Trakehner Breed

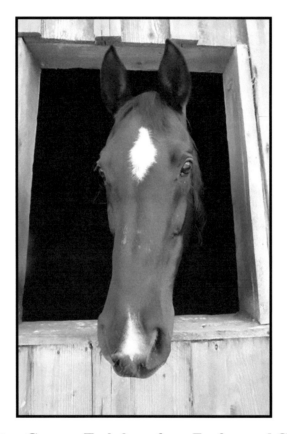

Firestar, German Trakehner from Fanfare and Carino

Through the beginning coincidence of Petrushka not being able to travel to the US a different path opened. The fortunate opportunity of finding her a new home began her exchange with a Trakehner mare. With the exception of the two thoroughbreds, the horses were Andalusian or Lusitano. This change now began a new chapter into the breed of warmbloods.

Most of my experience was in the art of riding, so the particulars of breeding while interesting wasn't a major focus. All of the horses had exceptional breeding in their own type but this wasn't as important as their athletic abilities. This path of having Fanfare join the group, started a new beginning.

To quote the opening sentence on the International Trakehner's page, "The Trakehner horse is the oldest warmblood breed in the world with a history spanning almost 300 years to the foundation of the main stud Trakehnen in 1732"(Trakehners International, 2013). Since I now had a Trakehner, finding out about this background became significant, because eventually we decided to breed her.

The Trakehner breed nearly ended with the horrific loss during the end of WWI. During the next years the breed began to reestablish when again the horses were being used in WWII as cavalry mounts. The details of their tragic demise are extremely hard to review. One of the virtually critical events was the evacuation of the Trakehner Stud between January 1945 and March 1945. There are historic accounts of the heroic efforts that made the difference in their survival. The stud which was in East Prussia is now in West Germany. It is an incredible miracle that out of 1,000 horses at Trakehnen only approximately 100 remained at the end of the war.

This fantastic historical background is the setting that revealed Fanfare's noble ancestry. At the time that Petrushka and Fanfare traded places, her new German family were to discover Petrushka's famous racing background and I the origin of Fanfare. Petrushka was a famous papered Thoroughbred offspring, so she would be an asset to the Trakehner breeding program because of the infusion of recognized Thoroughbreds and Arabians. On our side of the Atlantic, Fanfare's famous parents consisted of the stallion Harnish. Upon becoming more interested in the history of my horses, I searched many documents. One of the resources was the book, *The Trakehner*. The book has the entire important historical breed basis but also lists descriptions of the changes in the breed characteristics and the breeding horses which represented these qualities. According to the authors von Velsen-Zerweck and Schulte (1990), the Trakehner breed underwent several changes. The emphasis on military mounts now moved toward the emerging qualities of "riding horse qualities" (p. 32).

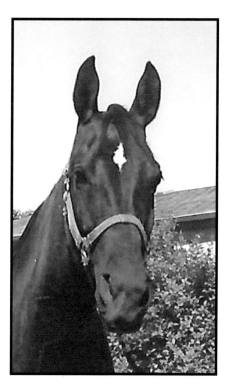

Fanfare, the last foal from the famous Trakehner stallion Harnish. The likeness to Star is striking

Merely by a series of chance occurrences I began a line of Trakehners for dressage training. The first was to be Fanfare von Harnish (as her newly American Trakehner papers translated from her German papers stated), for a much heftier sum than any of the fees paid in Europe. When the plans changed with an undiscoverable unsoundness preventing Fanfare's continued dressage training, a sad change happened to the Waldfriedhof riding and breeding establishment in Germany with the loss of the stallion Harnish. The last breeding line of the famous stallion was now in the United States.

Just as the tragedies of war have impacted horses, the less noticeable happenings subtly impact their owners. To accomplish an outstanding breeding farm, it takes an enormous amount of not only money but training talent. Besides selecting by looks, the other aspects of riding and temperament are important. These days it isn't a task that may easily be accomplished because of the inconsistency in the ongoing economy.

CHAPTER 34

Pavarotti and Smetterling

Pavie and Smetterling- best friends

The farm was now running smoothly and new stalls had been built, so it was time for more horses. The idea was to return to Germany and purchase two more Trakehners from the original farm that now had Petrushka and where the lovely Trakehner mare was born.

The foolish idea was to train them and eventually sell them. Ernie knew all along I could never part with an animal unless it was an impossible situation and I would go to great lengths to find as perfect a situation as possible. With Petrushka, her life was almost as close as I could have provided. Petrushka was in a riding school just as Primo and adored by her serious student riders. Both Primo and Petrushka had reached the higher levels competing in dressage and were easy to handle. Jeff pointed out with his vast experience that Primo would have a very good life in the consistency as a school horse. If it weren't that I respected Jeff so greatly I probably wouldn't have made the arrangement.

Returning to the same farm was fun and so was reuniting with Petrushka. I rode her several times and she was still the same wonderful horse I had left five years ago. It was heartwarming to see how well she looked, but at the same time it reminded me of the painful experience of finding out she couldn't return to the US. Yet now there was the possibility of two young geldings that were for sale. I rode both of them and they were excellent in their athletic ability, but still being young lacked what would take more training. Only being three years old they were very easygoing in temperament. This was most likely because of all the handling of the serious young German riders who not only cared for the horse they rode but an additional young horse. Both Germany and England have a regimented riding program that puts the rider through a series of skills before they gallop off into the sunset. The students diligently practice what most would call boring exercises under the careful eye of a serious trainer.

One of the purchased horses was the beautiful classic black Trakehner. It wasn't that he was wanting in conformation and movement that he didn't make the stallion grade but that he was eventually gelded because of the physical rigors of passing the stallion testing. This arduous testing, unknown to us and later discovered, caused him to have a suspensory ligament problem. The other bay-colored horse that had also received his Trakehner brand wasn't the knock out gorgeous type of his brother and didn't undergo the physically demanding training. When I rode him, I saw potential for an excellent national level horse quality. For what he lacked in beauty he would make up in his steadfast character. The famous Olympics horse of Podhajsky of the Austria Spanish Riding School succeeded even though he wasn't considered the breed type. There are several examples that counter the popular view of the outstandingly beautiful horse, of horses that rise to exceptional mounts due to less obvious factors.

This flight from Frankfurt was supervised with the owners who wanted to vacation in the States. The horses had an easy trip to their new home as we made one overnight stop to assure we didn't have a repeat of what happened with Fanfare on her long trip without a rest stop. They made a fine transition and the training had begun. Smetterling, the beautiful black, was especially talented and was making good progress to compete. We even met my German coach Gerd Reuter, at a local riding clinic. Since his visit to our farm, his reputation grew and he was sought to do several clinics at neighboring barns. We were happy to see he was making such a successful transition with his move from Germany. He had several horses winning at top competitions. He was so well-known in Germany since he had won several top competitions as a youth rider, sometimes it's difficult to make this transition as a business. He also was importing German warmbloods. Unfortunately, once again the horse industry was dependent on the outcome of poor economics.

The impact is a slow, insidious, progressive loss of all the things that support taking care of horses: veterinarians, farriers, feed stores, availability of hay, horse events, boarding barns, and especially part-time jobs for young people who want to learn about the horse industry. Since the horses were not our main business we were able to weather the ups and downs. The interesting fact was that these difficulties with the horses weren't limited but extended to our area of the aviation industry.

Pavie, as we nicknamed him and Smetterling were the beginning of the new horse activities, so now there were four adult horses, including Xierxo and Fanfare. Several years later the three horses still remaining on the farm were born. The farm became an enjoyable place to come home to and even though there were difficulties, they were easier to handle because it was ours and it was the end of the constant looking for a place to board the horses. Even with the present hay shortage because of several economic factors, they were surmountable with great extra effort.

Pavie became a remarkable horse as a schoolmaster. He unbelievably could be ridden by an advanced rider and perform medium difficulty exercises, yet have a totally inexperienced rider in a school lesson on the classical training on the long line. He became beloved to many riders who felt totally at ease on his back even though he was fairly large. He gave such a calm feeling to the rider they soon forgot his size. He was amazingly smooth in his transitions, so when the student had to learn to canter they weren't concerned about the moment of change from the two-beat trot into the three-beat canter. Most of the time the students didn't even know Pavie was cantering and would call out how wonderful it was. He was as talented as many of the schoolmasters I saw in England and Germany that were used to safely begin young riders. He performed as his schoolmaster colleagues and totally responded to the sound of the trainer. Even my advanced students noticed how much the horses listen to the sound of my voice.

One of Pavie's devotees was a young woman who loved horses and helped out with daily chores. She was indispensable in her ability to quietly help us care for the horses. There are many horse devotees that don't necessarily want to ride but love being around the quiet, tolerant horses that have been handled without roughness. Despite what many people think, horses actually have to learn to do all the horrible things people ascribe to them. After watching some of the longe lessons, she was so impressed she came to me and asked me if I would teach her. Since I didn't accept any compensation, I never turned any sincerely interested horse lover down. This student explained that she wanted to overcome her fear, because as a youngster she had been turned free on a supposedly calm horse only to have him become scared and bolts toward a barbed wire fence. She fell and was dragged, caught by the stirrup, toward the fence when suddenly her foot released. I assured her that all of our stirrups had break-away sides and that we would only do a walk lesson until she felt she was ready to continue. Needless to say she eventually, over a period of several months, was able to not only walk, but trot and canter. This was probably one of the best and happiest gifts among all the riders Pavie helped train.

Smetterling also was ridden by advanced riders calmly and taught them many advanced skills. He also was easy to ride. Perhaps the difference was that Smetterling wanted the rider to be knowledgeable about what to tell him and Pavie just seemed to know if it was a beginning rider. Possibly this might be because of my close presence with beginners he knew he had to follow my directions. The interesting fact was that when one of my advanced riders rode him in several competitions, he took directions totally from her. He looked like a different horse ridden by her. Pavie even helped her decide which boyfriend to pick. She was only finishing high school and wisely was mostly interested in her own horse and riding. When she began to prepare Pavie for competition, she invited one of her boyfriends to watch her ride. He had to be dragged from his truck and then sullenly sat by the side of the arena totally uninterested—he couldn't even fake it. The next time she came to ride Pavie, she had a new boyfriend with her. He sat down next to me as she elegantly rode Pavie to practice for the upcoming competition. The new boyfriend quietly asked questions and was able to see the art and skills it took to ride in this manner. Now happily married and three sons much later, she said Pavie helped her make her decision to marry the boyfriend who liked Pavie.

Looking back, I took a chance and made a deal to take both Pavie with his beautiful brother. The sellers saw this as an opportunity to rid themselves of a horse they didn't think they could sell. In retrospect, there was certainly wonderful providence that Pavie found his home on the farm.

CHAPTER 35

More Great Danes

Harley and Henry

We realized that we had to find a companion for Sebastian. Finally finding a Great Dane rescue group in Idaho, the arrangements were made to visit their foster home in Eastern Washington.

The appointment was made and Sebastian was ensconced comfortably in the back of the SUV and we proceeded to drive about three hours across Washington. At last, we reached the kennels where we were to meet a potential companion. After we met the owner of the kennel and Sebastian was introduced, we met a beautiful black-and-white Great Dane. She seemed somewhat subdued, but that is often the outcome of kenneling dogs. Everything was perfectly clean but to house so many dogs necessitated some schedule of exercise, feeding, and cleaning. It was decided that the new Great Dane, of about eighteen months old, named Harley, would be brought outside and we would take Sebastian to a meeting on neutral ground.

Sebastian was put on his leash and we walked to where the beautiful, alert female Great Dane stood. If we had any trepidation about this meeting, it was over in seconds. The two tails beat happy rhythms as we now let them meet. The transaction was now made as Sebastian turned toward the SUV and Harley followed, pulling her handler along. Sebastian now jumped into the back and Harley followed. They settled themselves in the back of the SUV, as if they had known each other forever. The kennel owner for the rescue shelter stated the obvious that this seemed to be a perfect home for Harley.

This was another incredible period on the farm and Sebastian and Harley both lived to the impossible Great Dane age of thirteen wonderful years. They had a wonderful life running free and were well-behaved with the horses, which is how this Great Dane adventure had begun so long ago in Spain with Tikki running on the beach with Shenandoah. There were several other Great Danes on the farm but none as indomitable as the present Great Dane Allie. The following story was published in my book *Positive Horses* and is an example of the sterling character of Great Danes.

This story was from my book that focused on behavioral positive methods of training horses. After we had unsuccessfully tried to rescue a Great Dane because they said we had horses, I found a black Great Dane that looked just like the beautiful black Spanish Great Dane Tikki. I wouldn't have thought that looking on the Internet was the best way to find a Great Dane, but it turned out to be perfect. I found a wonderful breeder who personally handled her Danes the way I treat my horses; we still communicate. The full story was included in my horse training book, because the positive methods used with horses are easily applied to dogs. To summarize, Allie had to be kept safe so she could freely go on excursions on the thirty-five acres that included a manmade canal that had deep sides and might be dangerous to slip into, so I always had a long cotton rope on the ATV. She had to immediately come on the command "Allie-Allie." The story is interesting about how we slowly conditioned the six-month-old Allie to walk along with an ATV, and finally run. She soon ran faster than I could safely drive the ATV but came anytime I yelled "Allie-Allie." This was wonderful as Allie loved running in the fields that often became wetland. The story continued until the two and-a-half-year-old Allie weighed 180 pounds and could run over twenty-five miles an hour over any surface, including the wetland that ran along the path.

This story happened in January just at sunset:

Allie and I are finishing our run and have stopped along the canal to enjoy the scenery on the other side. It has turned dark and the moon is beautifully reflected on the wetland field. We are heading back on the dry side of the canal. Allie is sitting right next to me when I see she is intently staring across the canal to the far trees next to the shining wetland field. She sees something and I strain to see what Allie is staring at in the far distance when an ominous dark cloaked figure suddenly appears at the edge of the distant trees and the lumbering figure starts splashing, wading through the wet field carrying a huge sack. The figure is totally unaware he's being watched and tracked by a huge dog that is larger than a male black panther.

The rest of this story unfolds in split seconds. Allie in her time with us hardly barks more than a one-bark notice and has never shown any aggressive behavior. I could hardly believe what happened next. This dark figure is a duck poacher who is setting decoys for an early morning hunt poaching on our property. As I yell, "Get off our property!" I realize that Allie is barking furiously, growling, and to my horror is airborne soaring over the canal. I anticipate pulling her out of the canal but my fears are allayed as I see her running, hardly touching the water and closing now within seconds to the dark retreating figure, who realizes he is being chased and frantically is trying to reach the barbed wire fence that he cut. Allie has covered what would be a deep-water covered football field in seconds. She is within several yards from the poacher when I grasp I cannot let her take this figure down for several reasons—mostly her safety. She is going to defend me at all cost; I can hear it in her continued angry barking as she pursues this fiend. This frantically stumbling, cumbersomely dressed poacher knows this isn't a miniature birddog chasing him and probably can't imagine what animal can run across eight to ten inches of water that fast. At the top of my lungs I yell the cue, "Allie-Allie!" In midair Allie turns and starts running back to me. I stay put and keep calling to her when out of the darkness she flies back across the canal and is sitting next to me looking expectantly with her cute, soft, puppy-like eyes as if to say, "Well, where's my treat?" I exhale and reach in my pocket and hand her a treat. Everything is as it was —a beautiful quiet evening, with a splendid moon shining over the wetland (Dammier, 2019, p. 103).

Even though we may not recognize them, there are strong bonds that we have created with both horses and dogs, which have become just as strong as the behavior we teach them; this is called our relationship, created by all the positive times of being together.

CHAPTER 36

Fanfare Finds a Farrier

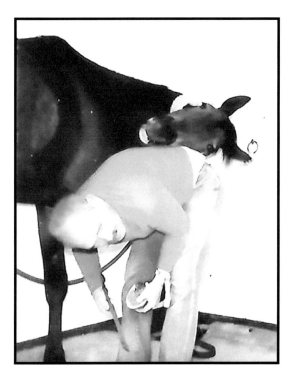

Let me rest my head!

Every horse owner's worst fears are not being able to find a farrier. Much of a horse's health depends on their hoofs. A farrier often solves many problems by discovering a hoof problem. It's hard to believe that an animal that big is totally vulnerable by what happens to their hoof. Petrushka during the time we were competing went through several episodes of being lame. The veterinarian looked at several possibilities in her shoulder and leg. This periodic soreness went on for almost a year before an experienced farrier who serviced most of the competitive horses on the national Spanish circuit, discovered she had an abscess concealed below the hoof wall. This would be as if you walked around with an uncomfortable pair of shoes on and developed a blister—it's excruciating. And so it was with poor Petrushka. As soon as the pressure was released, her recovery was miraculous. Farriers now attend sophisticated schools and understand and solve many complicated hoof difficulties with technology.

Farriers are often independent folks who frequently become extremely hard to contact even with today's cell phones. And like doctors, they have their appointment books filled up. Heavens forbid that like getting sick, your horse has a problem with their hoof and needs an appointment in between those tightly scheduled times that you've anxiously secured. Most horse owners don't let their farrier leave until they have secured the next appointment; they pray they don't have a hoof emergency.

All throughout our travels we've always worried about how we would find the next vet or farrier. In Spain, it became necessary to learn the art of hoof trimming so we could always have trimmed hoofs and happy horses. One of the horse club members was a farrier back in Texas before he joined the navy. When Dave found out about our problem, he convinced us that unless we really wanted to put on shoes that what he could teach us would help keep our horses with healthy hoofs. These lessons in trimming horse hoofs became necessary after the inexperienced Spanish farrier put a nail in the sensitive hoof area of one of the horses. This horse wasn't about to let a farrier near his hoof. Besides the problem of not being able to phone anyone in the southern most part of Spain, the farrier business was rough stuff. It mostly consisted of nailing a shoe on and cutting the hoof to fit. Dave imparted all the wonderful techniques he had learned in a Texas farrier school. We were also convinced about the benefit of having the horses without shoes.

Everything was easier while the horses were in Germany with the technology, precise fitting of shoes, and handling of horses. The farrier who serviced the private equestrian center where the horses were boarded always had the best care, and we were able to retire our horse trimming skills for many years. Things seemed definitely better when arriving back in the United States because at least horse owners could try and call a farrier. That didn't mean you'd get a return call but at least there was the option of leaving many messages and the empty comfort that someone might call back. We again polished off our hoof trimming skills to make sure the horses needed minimum care. At least we had excellent footing and all the horses were barefoot—without metal shoes. A few foals later, there were too many hoofs to keep up with, so once again we were dependent on reliable hoof care.

Again we were on shaky grounds finding a farrier because our farrier increasingly had more business than he could handle. The horses had endured incompetent farriers running nails into their sensitive hoof, roughed them up without cause, and charge a small king's ransom.

The predominant economics always exaggerated what happened to horses. This happened when we returned to the US and again twenty years later. Presently we don't have enough folks interested in performing a difficult skilled job; there are so many easier jobs. Having farriers with more business than they can handle happened before, but this time the farrier had glorious visions of grandeur because he was working for the latest horse whisperer on the circuit. Apparently, the rest of the clients are only to provide an audience in between visits to the grand farm.

After suffering several missed appointments and no returned call to reschedule, uneasily it appeared our eight horses were merely something to do when not servicing the grand horseman. After trying to keep up with a full-time job teaching, keeping up with trimming eight horses didn't seem possible. I made several calls to horsey friends with no return calls until my mare Fanfare helped us out.

Fanfare, the beautiful Trakehner who made a long trip to reside in the US, produced several beautiful offspring, adding to the abundance of hoofs that needed care. It unexpectedly happened while on a visit to the farm of her favorite stallion. Unfortunately, she didn't get to meet him because breeding technology had progressed to make the process safer, even though "The Owner" thought this happened forty years ago with his stallion.

This farm was the home of the successfully competing dressage Hungarian stallion Wistar who was owned by my friend Charlene Summers. During the time that I was busily riding and training horses in Europe, Charlene was beginning breeding a fine line of horses on a small farm and later a larger place. Since she didn't have an indoor arena on her original farm, several of her stallions visited us to practice in a new environment. One of my last visits with her happened by chance. Since she lived nearby, I decided to take a break with my hectic schedule and run over to see her. It was a fortuitous decision and I arrived as Charlene awaited the birth of her last foal that she bred before she sold her farm. We didn't have to wait long when soon that most beautiful filly was presented.

Charlene's last foal before she retired

On this day's visit, Fanfare's halter failed and we had to borrow one to use; Charlene provided it. Fanfare made her appointment and was loaded into the trailer for the short trip just down the road. We made the short trip and pulled up to the iron gate of the farm to observe that an unknown truck had pulled in behind us. I got out of our truck and a young man rolled down his window and pleasantly called, "I think this fell off your truck down the road." He described a stretch of road just after we made a turn onto the main highway where we live. We instantly remembered the broken halter placed on the back of the truck and forgotten that he held out to us. We pulled the truck and trailer through the gate, allowing his truck to follow us into the farm. As he turned his truck around, I noticed the writing on the side of his truck and noticed it was set-up as a farrier truck. I don't know what prompted me, but I immediately jumped out of the truck to the surprise of my husband.

I ran after the retreating truck and yelled, "Are you a farrier?" Since it was summer, he had his window opened and heard my call. He stopped the slowly moving truck and searched around for his card that he handed me through the open window. I thanked him and put the card safely in my pocket as he drove out the automatic iron gate that unhurriedly swung open and then closed. A few weeks later when the farrier scheduling had deteriorated and we were back filing hoofs, I found the business card of our mystery farrier and called. Amazingly, a live voice answered and we set up an appointment for the following week. This was great news…too good to be true.

The next week came and I breathed a sigh of relief as all the horses met their new farrier and calmly had their hoofs trimmed. It was a relief to know the horses would have regular trims. It was like a huge weight fell away; there was one less concern with the horses.

It's a mystery how Fanfare broke her halter but it certainly seems that there were several strange coincidences that worked in our favor. It is illogical that Fanfare could have anything to do with the timing of these events, but we certainly won't look a gift horse in the mouth!

CHAPTER 37

Wembley Has a Fan in West Berlin

The famous horse show of Jerez de la Frontera

Life on Monolo's farm had become peaceful and quiet with serious training, because "The Owner" was in hiding from various customs agencies. The Portuguese master came to visit and brought another famous classical trainer by the name Dr. Guilherme Borba. During one of the visits, I rode the beautiful Lusitano stallion that had been trained in Portugal by my coach. The horse world is a mini community of people devoted to horses, and besides running into people you know there will assuredly be horses. I had ridden both these wonderful stallions that were sold and ended up at Monolo's farm. Today I was to ride Wembley so famous classical trainer Borba could see him and Francisco's enduring work. We were inside the farm's small arena and reviewing the video tapes that Ernie took so I could review the lesson. It was hard to hear anything but the incessant crowing of the roosters but this didn't matter. This was the spring *feria* time in Spain and the horses were to be readied not only for breeding, but also for dressage competitions.

Horse travel is much easier with the new horsebox

By this time we owned our own serious horse transport. A company in North Dakota built a large stall-type insert that sits on the back of the large Ford truck and was designed to travel where a smaller horse trailer couldn't easily go. We were protected from the impounding of our horse rig, which happened to our Swedish friends we knew from the dressage circuit. She and her retired airline pilot husband lived in Estepona. She and I would be competing in dressage competitions, while her husband and Ernie would discuss all the inside information about aviation. Similar to horse members, the aviation groups are close-knit and supportive. The aviation people can talk freely about information, because they personally know all the players in this potentially dangerous profession.

Since our horse transport was a truck and not a vehicle with a trailer, it was spared from being impounded as our friends were. They suffered the humiliation of seeing their beautiful horse trailer at competitions being used by the Spanish military. During this time there were no European-type horse trailers in Spain. Even if you brought a European trailer in as a tourist, you would eventually run the risk of having it confiscated; this was true of campers too. The only reason we escaped was that all our vehicles were registered by the US military regulations. We had been laughed at with Shenandoah in her open truck with the side panels; no one was laughing at us now. The politics and economics drove every difficulty with horses, even horse transportation.

Instead of riding my own beautiful mares and being eliminated from winning, I now had what is know as *enchufe* riding Monolo's stallions and they won several places. My brilliant Portuguese trainer, Francisco had trained them all. If you think I felt as I was an injured party…you are wrong. One will always face difficulties in life and it's how one deals with them that makes the difference. I rode because I loved it and wanted to see if I could beat my own standards. It's the same reason that Ernie kept flying small planes after the exciting life of a fighter pilot; he wanted to fly ever since his mom let him take a demo ride at a county fair.

Wembley had performed quite well this time and placed third in dressage. As we were walking back to the stalls, a lady approached us and called, "He's a beautiful Lusitano… Am I right?" That started a conversation and friendship that brought us together many years later in West Berlin. She also had a Lusitano in Germany. We spent hours talking about this breed and training. I had no idea that we would meet again and under what unbelievable circumstances. At this time there was no thought that our lives would take us to Germany—another coincidence? "The incredible turn of the earth." This was Francisco's reaction upon hearing how far his training of Wembley had reached.

Ernie was happily enjoying teaching would-be pilots under the "severe clear skies" of Spain. Severe clear is an aeronautical expression that means no weather in sight and unlimited visibility.

The city of West Berlin played a particularly poignant role in that history. Ernie Dammier Aeronautical professors Steve O'Brien were teaching at the EC (Extended Campus) resident center at Templehof Weltflughafen ("airport"), only a few blocks from the Berlin Wall and a couple of kilometers from Checkpoint Charlie, when the Iron Curtain started crumbling and the Berlin wall fell.

(www.erau.edu/about/heritage.html)

And we were there in a hotel one block away!

CHAPTER 38

Fences Make Good Neighbors

Pavie had many friends

Until we owned the home in Germany we were always faced with close neighbors. The apartment we owned overlooking the Mediterranean was perfect…eleven months of the year. The eight floors were predominantly owned by Spaniards living in Seville who moved to the vacation apartment for their one month of vacation in August. So, the three other American families who also owned apartments had peace for eleven months. Luckily they left about the time that the school year began and we didn't have to worry that we would have to save one of their kids drowning at two a.m. in the unattended swimming pool.

In Germany, even when we temporally rented the little apartment in Ochsenfurt, our kitchen window was within an arm's reach of our friendly neighbor whom I spent many hours talking to through our open windows. Out cats would sit on their respective window sills eyeing each other. When we left, she presented us with a beautiful candle perched on a horseshoe; I still have it. I still have contact with many German friends and I'm sure it would be that way with the late Spanish family of Monolo and his wife Maria.

Now with thirty-five acres things would be perfect. This property was the main section of what had been one of the largest dairy farms in the area. The original owner now lived in a beautiful home to one side of the property that she had built when her husband passed away. When she found out I had lived in Germany and spoke German, I became friends with this lovely Austrian woman. Again, things are always in change and Hermina finally tired of the wet winters and moved to Arizona. She sold her beautiful European-styled home to the rough-edged chap, now our neighbor, who thought he was going to farm. His cows were always getting free to run down the state highway nearby. Cows are often difficult, so the cows suddenly disappeared.

Things went fine for a while and we put up with him stealing hay and poaching ducks. Since he didn't care about the quality of his hay, he didn't worry about the remains of gunshot as our hay cutter did. Ernie would always quietly discuss the hay problem and they would come to the conclusion that his hay crew has "mistakenly" taken hay off our property and return the hay. At this point there wasn't a fence separating the hay fields.

The new German youngsters, the Trakehner horses, had arrived and some of my students and I were having fun training them. Pavarotti and Smetterling, as they were named, were easy to work with because of the beginning handling with the young riders at the farm in Germany. Slowly we accustomed them to working in the indoor arena and then to the outdoor arena, so now it was time to start walks on the back hay fields.

Pavarotti, called Pavie for short, was about a half-year older and was less overly sensitive, so I began a short walk with him to the back of the property. We came to the back section that had many tall trees. The property was wonderful with all the animals that lived in the fields. As we approached the tallest tree near the woodland section that cornered the hay fields, a huge hawk suddenly flew out over us. I saw Pavie turn his head to see what was over us when suddenly he fell over, having lost his balance. He sat there on the ground stunned and I stepped off carefully and cautiously, allowing him to stand up. This time Pavie was safely up on the field without the slippery surface of the English lady's arena.

Riding on the cut fields of hay was wonderful and soon it was time for the more nervous brother Smetterling to accompany Pavie on a field walk. My friend Stacey, who was an excellent rider, accompanied me, her riding on Pavie and I riding the nervous Smetterling. Everything was perfect as we made the loop around the canal that divided the property in half and headed back to where we could see our husbands standing and watching us. Pavie led the way with Smetterling following his older, confident brother. Suddenly a truck appeared on the neighbor's field, most likely picking up more hay. Stacey and I continued riding toward the watching men when the truck started to rapidly drive at us, yelling to get off the field. Our husbands, immediately seeing what was happening, ran toward us yelling to the crazy truck driver to stop. Smetterling was nervous but stayed with Pavie. Pavie now turned and stood looking at the oncoming truck, not moving a bit. Smetterling nervously kept close with Pavie but it seemed he must have been saying, "Hey Pavie, should we run?" Pavie stood rigidly firm…almost daring the truck, which finally with the force of our husbands' presence suddenly turned back to retreat to his farm. Pavie stood firm and Stacey had the horse knowledge to know she was safe and could depend on him. Pavie was the quintessential war horse: calm and courageous under pressure. Pavie unquestionably had in his extensive Trakehner heritage a brave and daring warhorse.

The men went over to talk to the neighbor about what had happened. Seems this was a visitor who was helping bring in hay and didn't know that without the fence that the horses weren't on his land.

Needless to say, shortly thereafter a fence was built. As the famous poet Robert Frost said in his famous poem: "Good fences make good neighbors."

CHAPTER 39

Firebird: Hungarian

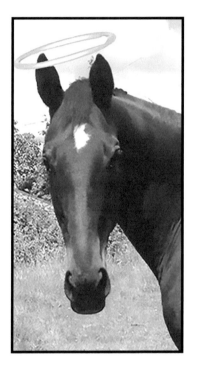

Firebird has an angelic face. Her photo was used for the book cover- *Positive Horses*

Sometimes bad luck turns into something unexpectedly wonderful because it opens a new opportunity. Because of the exceptional breeding possibility with the imported German Trakehner mare Fanfare after the Russian foal, the focus was to continue attempting to get to breed with European bred stallions, which is how the Trakehner stallion Carino came into the picture. My intent was to train Fanfare but she continued to be irregularly unsound. Her exercise program always began with her beautiful movement to sadly show a slight unsteady stride in her hind leg, so again we thought of breeding. Since my expertise wasn't in breeding, we relied on the farms specializing in the intricacies of bloodlines.

Fanfare had several hundred years of famous relatives as did Carino. The aging stallion unfortunately was getting older and even though we had successfully gained the Trakehner colt Firestar, the following year Carino's shipment wasn't usable for breeding. Timing is of the essence, and the expense of getting Fanfare ready for the occasion seemed as if it would be lost. Again, we were back at my friend Charlene's wonderful farm where she had a small lab set up near her kitchen. She worked together with a very competent veterinarian, who sadly has just retired with little opportunity to find the same quality. It's the new change from a single vet who worked alone to large vet associations making it more expensive to the horse owner. I knew him for almost twenty years and he made difficult times much easier.

Charlene studied the sample from Carino and announced the unfortunate news. She allowed me to look at the totally quiet slide where there should have been much movement. I was crestfallen when this opportunity seemed lost. Charlene then explained that my perfectly bred German mare would be a match for her Hungarian stallion and added many of the breeding facts that I had no knowledge of.

Not knowing anything about how several of these European bloodlines were connected, a new direction began with the breeding and successful foaling of the filly Firebird. The farm started a new chapter with an exceptional Hungarian mare. While researching the three youngsters' heredity, it became apparent that due to the struggles of war and economics, the lines of the Russian Orlov-Rostopchin, Trakehner, and Hungarian horses have common ancestry.

When reading the past history about these breeds, it's hard to comprehend the tragedies of not only the horses but their heroic owners who did everything to save them. In the book *The Heavenly Horses,* one of the moving stories is exemplified by a young lad who helps lead the way for a group of struggling Hungarian horses and carts escaping the approaching armies to the safety of the Austrian border and an example of the amazing courage needed (Weizel,1986). The next sequence reveals what also happened to many European horses, including the Hungarian horses when they were able to get the help they needed and to get the surviving Hungarian horses to the States. "The Lippizans were not the only horses rescued from the Russians in 1945 by the Third Army under the Command of General George Patton"(Weizel. 1986, p.53).

For non-horse experienced folks, the horse appears to have been nothing more than a means of transportation. So then, how could someone become deeply attached to a horse? Definitely it's different than our relationships with dogs but on a similarly less-complex means; they communicate in subtle ways only obvious to their owners. This is especially true because my horses have been in my care since their birth. Certainly, simpler and less complex than the communication with dogs—one only needs to pay attention to less obvious, elusive actions that rely on human interpretation. Animals learn intense and unique ways of communicating after being in a special relationship that exceeds what many would consider the limitations of animals.

The inability of many, including the press, to understand there might be more of an emotional attachment besides a single motivation of owning an "expensive horse" is dishearteningly absent in this typically characteristic press release about saving the horses fleeing the war. Their response denies that anyone would take all of their worldly resources and risk their own life to save a horse: "The press back in the States had discovered the army was shipping European horses to America and launched a tirade against taxpayers' money…" (Weizel, 1986, p. 56). Possibly this "discovering report" had the same lack of research that typifies the press in exciting readers negatively.

All three of the horses born on our farm had unique personalities. Both stallions were extremely easy to handle and responded very positively to the few known helpers who handled them—mostly me and my students. So, they were accustomed to consistent handling even though each had their own characteristics.

Firebird was now the only remaining mare along with the two stallions on the farm. She was doing extremely well being trained as a dressage horse until suddenly the normal shows were cancelled. We then returned to their program of classical long reining and slowly introduced them to the small training cart as outlined in my book *Positive Horses*. Firebird is pictured on the front cover wearing a halo photoshopped over her sweet-looking face. This was only to be for a short time and to keep everyone in work. Unfortunately, this has turned out to be a longer hiatus than planned. With an uncertain breeding future for horses that began in the economic difficulties beginning in 2008, it seemed fortunate that I didn't keep my promise to breed her.

CHAPTER 40

Back in the US

Happy in their own pasture

The big decision had been made to sell our beautiful German home that we planned to stay in. Things have a way of changing, especially when pressured by economics. Opportunities coalesced for Ernie to take a position as the head of the undergraduate aviation university program. I was at the end of finding a new boarding place and my German coach had just also made the decision to head out to the United States. It was time to consider having our own farm back home—wherever that was. We both had been overseas so long.

All organizations go through a similar program whereby they start with a praiseworthy mission and slowly are infiltrated by another group that begins to destructively implement their ideas, rather than starting their own group. It's pretty much stealing the hard work of the organization they attempt to grab. It is not different than the Ochsenfurt horse facility that began equitably with both jumping and dressage enthusiasts benefiting.

As the German economics during this period changed, the atmosphere of the riding establishment also changed. Several members, as well as I, had more than one horse boarded at the stable, but as the economy changed, those members sold their horses. Just before I left to fly the horses to the US, the numerous dressage owners who had several horses had left the club. The club was now predominantly the jumping group that left the jumps in the arena so it couldn't be groomed. Besides the indoor arena, the eventing group had a beautiful outdoor arena where the jumps remained permanently. The club previously had a Wednesday evening jump night so the horses could have indoor competitions and practice for coming events. The idea was that the jumps would be dismantled so the arena could be dragged and groomed. The arena caretaker quit because he could no longer groom the arena with the jumps, which now created deep ridges in the normally beautifully groomed smooth surface. Any organizational situation may be evaluated for the same difficulties—mission creep.

Moving to the US didn't stop these organizational conflicts but in regard to our horses, it was heaven; we now had our own farm. Horses were still the victim of politics and economics as we soon discovered. The economics was hitting horse owners as it recently happened in Germany for horse owners with less money for discretionary hobbies. With my part-time position as a military career counselor, the base daily bulletin published each day at our office cautioned military personnel on the range, where the military practiced live shooting, to be aware of horses that had been abandoned by their owners.

The fun part was the creating of a beautiful place where all the animals could be happy and continue training dressage horses, besides my new job teaching aviation psychology and working with graduates on their research projects.

With the many coincidences in life, we bred Fanfare with a lovely Russian stallion that had escaped a dire situation and was sold for very few dollars. Our lovely mare didn't stay without traces of lameness to be able to compete but was otherwise in perfect health, so by a chance situation we ended up with the farm's first foal. Fanfare never showed any discomfort but only when we began the systematic training program would she demonstrate an irregular step. We never found the reason for Fanfare's problem, but we guess it occurred in her arduous truck ride from the Los Angeles airport to Washington State. The veterinary technology has expanded and even in the last ten years assessment of difficult problems is more discoverable. The typical horse owner may even use the new DNA testing to understand hereditary health problems besides paternity.

Fanfare was a wonderful mother and the farm continued easily with the additional responsibility of youngsters. Both Fanfare and Xierxo, because of their friendship since being shipped together, were normally turned out together in the same pasture. They happily took on the role of parents with Firefox being born in the pasture with the pair. Because this turned out so positively, they continued their parental roles with the next two. We kept a continual vigil to assure that the relationship stayed safe. Amazing when each youngster behaved badly, the only admonishment from Fanfare or Xierxo was verbal. Neither one ever kicked or bit a disobedient youngster. We especially watched to assure that Xierxo didn't feel threatened by a young colt such as Firefox and later Firestar. It was wonderful having this baby-sitting service and each youngster stayed in this trio until they were nearly two years old. It was remarkable to witness these relationships, which with horses or any animals isn't always so devoted and should be carefully monitored. Interestingly, two of the youngsters, Firebird and Firestar, now more than fifteen, remain loyal companions having shared adjoining stalls. Now that Firestar is gelded, they may be pastured together. Horse relationships may be as difficult as humans but this one turned out fantastically.

Besides the military personnel finding abandoned horses, horses were also left in remote areas that were common to many areas in Washington State for trail riding. Positively however, all my horse friends that still are working with horses continue and merely adjust, even my contacts in Spain, Portugal, and Germany. While on a recent trip to Germany to attend the famous Frankfurter Buchmesse-Frankfurt Book Fair, the world's largest attendance of publishing companies and visitors to promote my other books, I had the option to revisit several familiar horse places, which was really the important part of the planned trip: Horses. It was hoped that I could again see the farm where my Trakehners originated.

The book fair was wonderfully organized and my attendance was coordinated with an American publisher that offered other published authors the opportunity to promote their books at this fair with their company display. I was one of the few authors who actually attended their exhibition of about fifty books. My purpose was to find out more about the publishing industry. Since my primary interest was in aviation research, the foray into regular publishing was to confirm what I already knew about the business. The books that I had already published about horses were merely to put ideas to paper for a diversion from the serious work of writing research proposals and helping students with their own research projects. Unless a publisher believes there is a great deal of money to made, one is merely a target of a deep hole to throw money into.

During the trip several of my aviation friends took me on a drive around Ochsenfurt. We had lunch in a small restaurant on the main street where Ernie and I often enjoyed the huge plates of German food and local wine and beer. The Ochsenfurt beer still is procured using the sugar beets from the farm where we temporality boarded and enjoyed outdoor rides, Ernie on his mountain bike and me with the nervous Xierxo. As we sat in the outdoor garden it was as if nothing had changed. It was as if we had only walked out of the cute little apartment we rented in the town while our house was being built to have dinner; it was not more than around the corner. It was truly unreal sitting there in the garden with my friends. The almost three decades melted away.

Hardly anything had changed in Ochsenfurt and the old Roman bridge was still used. Because of some of the newer roads, we had difficulty finding the riding club but it was still there. When we arrived, a young group of students were excitedly talking about their new dressage instructor as the day's sessions had just ended. We looked in the arena and besides looking slightly older than I remembered, we noticed the footing had recently been groomed and watered! The Ochsenfurt club was once again seriously involved with dressage.

Sadly, the other breeding and riding establishment, Waldfriedhof, at the edge of Würzburg, no longer exists and a large shopping establishment equivalent to the Home Depot has taken over what were large fields, a large barn, and outdoor arena. Over twenty-six years ago this barn had not only a Trakehner breeding program with the famous stallion Harnish, but also an inexpensive riding school for youngsters. Three of the horses that had lived on our farm in Washington came from this farm. It shouldn't have been a surprise because this was over thirty years ago; the horses that we had purchased had passed away more than fifteen years ago. This missing piece of returning to Ochsenfurt was a cheerless reminder of passing time and how things change.

Horse lovers still face many problems from the economic downturn in 2008, which not only changed the horse industry but all the fun activities such as boating, aviation, and others. Once more many preparations for competing with the three remaining horses came to an end with recent horse show cancellations.

Most stories will come to an end but optimistically a new chapter continues and is still being written. The three horses born on the farm are in excellent training but now age wise are getting to the point that the demands of competitive travel would not be easy for them or even feasible with the present economic situation. Horse enthusiasts who traveled a reasonable distance to attend horse shows now find this financially impossible.

Celebrating a career change!

Life is a series of decisions, so the horses are doing something I had experienced in Europe: Driving. Having learned the European art of classical long reining, we have returned to this art with all three horses again, which they all know because it was the safe method to put them under saddle as youngsters. Even though these three are much more talented as dressage horses, we've successfully taught them to pull the training cart that was so much enjoyed with Pavie. We cleaned up the cart, pumped up the bicycle tires, and began with Firefox. After all, historically the Orlov-Rostopchin line can be traced back during the Russian Count Rostopchin horse breeding time, whose horses were known for the fast, flashy horses with sleek carriages. Firefox is living up to his heritage driving the small cart; now we only have to find him the flashy carriage. The three are talented dressage horses and can easily be returned to their mounted training. Teaching them all to drive is another fun equestrian discipline that only makes them more versatile.

Even though some of the planned stories have ended, new chapters are still being written by many loving horse owners. This last chapter considers all those dedicated horse folks who kept an eye optimistically on a potential future through hope and their dedication even through unimaginable hardships. And as a devoted horse friend adding a valuable thought said, "Looking for a little bit of joy each day with our beloved horses." We all do this and continue…**all for the love of horses**.

AFTERWORD

This story is about all the wonderful animals and people that comprise over thirty-five years traveling through Europe to return to our farm in the United States. It has been reflective to review all the cheerful and funny stories but unsettling to view the happenings in a historical perspective. While reviewing the research about the Hungarian horses' story about their escape to safety, it appears that once again, horses are suffering the consequences of war but again there are heroic people are saving them… so the story will continue.

The photographs in this book are designed to convey the various light-hearted moments but also the part of dedication that it takes to accomplish any difficult skill. Many of the people described, were not only dedicated to the equestrian art but also to the well-being of their partners. The trainers who I was fortunate to work with performed as they would with any dancer; the horses always responded in kind. It is with this end that this book was written.

POSTSCRIPT

Since the writing of this book several interesting stories could be included. Regrettably our veterinarian, Dr. Best, of over fifteen years retired having helped us successfully breed three horses. His calm placid demeanor will be missed. Our past veterinarian Dr. Grubb has a new location nearer to the farm and has already helped Firefox through a neurological problem. Firefox is slowly resuming work and hopefully soon will be pulling his cart.

Along with the necessary horse assistance is the farrier. Steve has had to retired from the stress of the hard work of working with hoofs. He and his wife are still visitors on the farm and Steve is always available for horse knowledge from his many years of experience. After a few false starts, we finally found Emily on a list at the local farrier supply store. The horses all love her because of her easy manner. She caught the seriousness of Firefox's problem, and alerted me it wasn't a simple hoof soreness. She even has a pink hoof jack stand and is an avid three-day eventer, which gives her an understanding of larger warmbloods.

My two dressage students Nikki and Krista are working hard to raise their families of energetic boys. While we're all disappointed in not preparing the horses for continued dressage work…things happen, and change. Krista helps during the week and has been valuable spotting potential problems. Farms always need someone experienced who can jump in and help, and they both certainly helped in several horse episodes.

Several of the stories recount many of the horse lovers' selfless thoughtfulness. There are countless people that in small ways helped make all this possible through acts of kindness.

REFERENCES

Timeline of Chinese Dynasty (n.d.).
(https://www.chinafetching.com/timeline-of-chinese-dynasty

Dammier, P. (2019). *Positive horses* Bloomington,Indiana: Iuniverse.
Embry Riddle Aeronautical University.(n.d.). http://www.erau.edu/about/heritage.html

Google Earth (n.d.). https://earth.google.com/web/search/
El+Rocio,+Spain

Kawsar, I.(n.d.). *Lipizzan Horse: A horse dedicated to Spanish Riding School in Vienna.* https://
www.thevetexpert.com/

Oelke, H. (n.d.). Sorraia Information site http://www.sorraia.org/ruy-d-andrade.html

Oliveira, N. (1982). *Notes and reminiscences of a Portuguese rider.* (n.p.).

Oliveira, P. & Costa, E. (2012). *Portuguese school of equestrian art.* Franktown, VI: Xenophon
Press LLC.

Magnus, A.(1979). *Several steeds shine in soggy saddle show.* The Jack Tar. p. 9.

Map of Ming Tombs. (n.d.). https://www.beijingservice.com/beijing-map/ming-tomb-map.jpg

Podhajsky, A. (1967). My horses, my teachers. Garden City, New York: Doubleday & Company, Inc.

Jerez-Xeres (2014). Bodegas: Fernando A. Terry. http://Jerez-Xeres-Sherry: Bodegas: Fernando
A de Terry

The Russian Crisis (2013). RaboResearch
The Russian Crisis 1998 - RaboResearch http://www.rabobank.com

Trakehners International (2013). The history of the Trakehner horse
http://www.trakehnersinternational.com/history/index.html

Vavra, R. (1883). Unicorns I have known. New York, N.Y.: William Morrow and Company, Inc.

Von Velsen-Zerweck, Dr. Eberhard & Schulte, E.(1990). The Trakehner. London: J.A. Allen and Company.

Williams, J.(1996). Doñana National Park https://www.andalucia.com/environment/protect/don
 Ruy d' Andrade Sorraia. (n.d.). http://www.sorraia.org/ruy0d0dandrade.html

Starozhilovsky Stud Farm,(1993). History of the Ryazan Territory: Starozhilovsky Stud Farm. (*
 The material from this webpage is presently unavailable.)

Wildlife Conservation Society. (2008). Massive Crocodile Training at the Bronx Zoo.
 https://www.youtube.com/watch?v=cql6nlRWvCA

Weisel, Virginia Johnson,(1986). The heavenly horses. Missoula, Mt. Mountain Press.

INDEX

ABOUT THE AUTHOR

Patti Dammier has been an educator of horses and riders for over thirty-five years. Her experience both in the United States and Europe provides a broad equestrian perspective. During twenty-three years overseas, while teaching elementary school, she studied equestrian disciplines in Spain, Germany, Portugal, and England. Many of the story situations described in this book are based on her true-life experiences.

As an equestrian having trained and competed in Europe, Dr. Patricia (Patti) Dammier, with a PhD in psychology, uses her expertise to write about horse training based on scientific theories and educational methods. While studying dressage in Europe, she had several opportunities to work with driving carriages. Even though this wasn't her primary interest, when she returned to the US, she began to teach one of her dressage horses to drive a small cart. Because of this experience, she has promoted several stories about driving carts/carriages. In a fiction story about *Summer Fun and Driving Carriages* and her nonfiction book, *Positive Horses,* she includes information about driving carts/carriages with horses. Also included is information about para-driving, which allows horse enthusiasts with disabilities that would prevent them from mounting horses the ability to drive a cart/carriage.

Besides being involved with horse training, Patti is a consummate researcher and involved with many aspects of writing research reports from aviation human factors to behavioral science. It's with a researcher's perspective that she looks at her nonfiction and fiction writing. Although some of the story depictions are fictionalized, the research behind them is grounded in science. (www.GotCarrots.com)

Xierxo and Patti Barcelona

Printed in the United States
by Baker & Taylor Publisher Services